WITH THE BOER FORCES

WITH THE BOER FORCES

HOWARD C. HILLEGAS

AUTHOR OF OOM PAUL'S PEOPLE AND CORRESPONDENT OF
THE NEW YORK WORLD

CruGuru

WITH THE BOER FORCES

ISBN: 978-1-920265-12-0

First published in 1900 by Methuen & Co
This edition published in 2008 by CruGuru.com
www.cruguru.com

COMMANDANT-GENERAL LOUIS BOTHA

About the Author

Howard C. Hillegas: 30 December 1872 – 29 January 1918

Howard Clemens Hillegas, author and traveler, and for ten years a member of the editorial staff of The New York Herald, was born in Pennsburg, Penn. on 30 December 1872, a son of Dr. John Gery Hillegas and Catherine Ziegler Hillegas. He was a descendant of Michael Hillegas, first Treasurer of the United States. He graduated from Franklin and Marshall College in 1894, and in the following year he came to New York, joining the staff of The New York World.

In 1895 he was sent to South Africa as a correspondent of The New York World. He was the first correspondent to announce that the fighting between the British and the Boers had commenced in the Anglo-Boer War (1899 - 1902). Mr. Hillegas, who had been a close friend of Boer President Paul ("Oom Paul") Kruger, published a book entitled "Oom Paul's People" in 1899. In 1900 his book "With the Boer Forces" was published.

On his return from a trip around the world in 1901, Mr. Hillegas published and edited The Saratoga Sun. Next he was a member of the staffs of The New York World and The Evening World, and in 1906 joined The New York Herald, on which he became successively night city editor, day city editor, city editor, and editorial writer.

About five months before his death from pneumonia in 1918, Mr. Hillegas resigned from The New York Herald to become associate editor of The Hotel Reporter. At the time of his death he lived in New Brighton, Staten Island.

Preface

In the following pages I have endeavoured to present an accurate picture of the Boers in war-time. My duties as a newspaper correspondent carried me to the Boer side, and herein I depict all that I saw. Some parts of my narrative may not be pleasing to the British reader; others may offend the sensibilities of the Boer sympathisers. I have written truthfully, but with a kindly spirit and with the intention of presenting an unbiased account of the struggle as it was unfolded to the view from the Boer side. I shall be criticised, no doubt, for extolling certain virtues of the Boers, but it must be noticed that their shortcomings are not neglected in these lines.

In referring to Boer deeds of bravery I do not mean to insinuate that all British soldiers were cowards any more than I mean to imply that all Boers were brave, but any man who has been with armies will acknowledge that bravery is not the exclusive property of the peoples of one nation. The Boers themselves had thousands of examples of the bravery of their opponents, and it was not an extraordinary matter to hear burghers express their admiration of deeds of valour by the soldiers of the Queen. The burghers, it may be added, were not bitter enemies of the British soldiers, and upon hundreds of occasions they displayed the most friendly feeling toward members of the Imperial forces. The Boer respected the British soldier's ability, but the same respect was not vouchsafed to the British officer, and it was not unreasonable that a burgher should form such an opinion of the leaders of his enemy, for the mistakes of many of the British officers were so frequent and costly that the most unmilitary man could easily discern them. On that account the Boers' respect for the British soldier was not without its mixture of pity.

There are those who will assert that there was no goodness in the Boers and that they conducted the war unfairly, but I shall make no attempt to deny any of the statements on those subjects. My sympathies were with the Boers, but they were not so strong that I should tell untruths in order to whiten the Boer character. There were thieves among them--I had a horse and a pair of field-glasses stolen from me on my first journey to the front--but that does not prove that all the Boers were wicked. I spent many weeks with them, in their laagers, commandos, and homes, and I have none but the happiest recollections of my sojourn in the Boer country. The generals and burghers, from the late Commandant-General Joubert to the veriest Takhaar, were extremely courteous and agreeable to me, and I have nothing but praise for their actions. In all my experiences with them I never saw one maltreat a prisoner or a wounded man, but, on the contrary, I observed many of their acts of kindness and mercy to their opponents.

I have sought to eliminate everything which might have had a bearing on the causes of the war, and in that I think I have succeeded. In my former book, dealing with the Boers in peaceful times, I gave my impressions of the political affairs of the country, and a closer study of the subject has not caused me to alter my opinions. Three years before the war began, I wrote what has been almost verified since--

"The Boers will be able to resist and to prolong the campaign for perhaps eight months or a year, but they will finally be obliterated from among the nations of the earth. It will cost the British Empire much treasure and many lives, but it will satisfy those who caused it, the South African politicians and speculators."

The first part of the prediction has been realised, but at the present time there is no indication that the Boer nation will be extinguished so completely or so suddenly, unless the leaders of the burghers yield to their enemy's forces before all their powers and means of resistance have been exhausted. If they will continue to fight as men who struggle for the continued existence of their country and government should fight, and as they have declared they will go on with the war, then it will be three times eight months or three times a year before peace comes to South Africa. Presidents Kruger and Steyn have declared that they will continue the struggle for three years, and longer if necessary. De Wet will never yield as long as he has fifty burghers in his commando, and Botha will fight until every British soldier has been driven from South African soil. Hundreds of the burghers have made even firmer resolutions to continue the war until their cause is crowned with victory. There may be some among them who fought and are fighting because they despise Britons and British rule, but the vast majority are on commando because they firmly believe that Great Britain is attempting to take their country and their government from them by the process of theft which we enlightened Anglo-Saxons of America and England are wont to style "benevolent assimilation." They feel that they have the right to govern their country in accordance with their own ideas of justice and equality, and, naturally, they will continue to fight until they are victorious, or might asserts itself over their conception of right. If they have the power to make Great Britain feel that their cause is just, as our forefathers in America did a hundred years ago, then the Boers have vindicated themselves and their actions in their own eyes and in the eyes of the world. If they lack in the patriotism which men who fight for the life of their country usually possess, then the Boers of South Africa will be exterminated from among the nations of the world and no one will offer any sympathy to them.

We Anglo-Saxons of America and Great Britain have a habit of calling our enemies by names which would arouse the fighting blood of the most peaceable individual, and when there is a Venezuelan question to be discussed we do not hesitate to practice this custom, born of our blood-alliance, by making each other the subjects of the vituperative attacks. During the Spanish-American war we made most uncomplimentary remarks concerning our short-lived enemy, and more recently we have been emphasising the vices of our *protégés*, the Filipinos, with a scornful disregard of their virtues. The Boers, however, have had a greater burden to bear. They have had cast at them the shafts of British vituperation and the lyddite of American venom. In a few instances the lyddite was far more harrowing than the shafts, and in the vast majority of instances both were born of ignorance. There are unclean, uncouth, and unregenerate Boers, and I doubt whether any one will stultify himself by declaring that there are none such of Britons and Americans. I have been among the Boers in times of peace and in times of war, and I have always failed to see that they were in any degree lower than the men of like rank or occupation in America or England. The farmers in Rustenburg probably never saw a dress suit or a *décolleté* gown, but there are innumerable regions in America and Great Britain where similarly dense ignorance prevails. I have been in scores of American and British homes which were not more spotlessly clean than some of the houses on the veld in which it was my pleasure to find a night's entertainment, and nowhere, except in my own home, have I ever been treated with more courtesy than that which was extended to me, a perfect stranger, in scores of daub and wattle cottages in the Free State and the Transvaal. I will not declare that every Boer is a saint, or that every one is a model of cleanliness or virtue, but I make bold to say that the majority of the

Boers are not a fraction less moral, cleanly, or virtuous than the majority of Americans or Englishmen, albeit they may be less progressive and less handsome in appearance than we imagine ourselves to be.

As I have stated, the politics of the war has found no part in the following pages, and an honest effort has been made to give an impartial account of the proceedings as they unfolded themselves before the eyes of an American. The struggle is one which was brought about by the politicians, but it will probably be ended by the layman who wields a sword, and who knows nothing of the intricacies of diplomacy. The Boers desire to gain nothing but their countries' independence; the British have naught to lose except thousands of valuable lives if they continue in their determination to erase the two nations. Unless the Boers soon decide to end the war voluntarily, the real struggle will only begin when the Imperial forces enter the mountainous region in the north-eastern part of the Transvaal, and then General Lucas Meyer's prophecy that the bones of one hundred thousand British soldiers will lay bleaching on the South African veld before the British are victorious may be more than realised.

One word more. The English public is generous, and will not forget that the Boers are fighting in the noblest of all causes--the independence of their country. If Englishmen will for a moment place themselves in the position of the Boers, if they will imagine their own country overrun by hordes of foreign soldiers, their own inferior forces gradually driven back to the wilds of Wales and Scotland, they will be able to picture to themselves the feelings of the men whom they are hunting to death. Would Englishmen in these circumstances give up the struggle? They would not; they would fight to the end.

HOWARD C. HILLEGAS.
NEW YORK CITY,
August 1, 1900.

Table of Contents

1. The Way to the Boer Country

Immediately after war was declared between Great Britain and the Boers of the Transvaal and the Orange Free State, the two South African republics became ostracised, in a great measure, from the rest of the civilised world. The cables and the great ocean steamship lines, which connected South Africa with Europe and America, were owned by British companies, and naturally they were employed by the British Government for its own purposes. Nothing which might in any way benefit the Boers was allowed to pass over these lines and, so far as it was possible, the British Government attempted to isolate the republics so that the outside world could have no communication of any sort with them. With the exception of a small strip of coast-land on the Indian ocean, the two republics were completely surrounded by British territory, and consequently it was not a difficult matter for the great Empire to curtail the liberties of the Boers to as great an extent as it was pleasing to the men who conducted the campaign. The small strip of coast-land, however, was the property of a neutral nation, and, therefore, could not be used for British purposes of stifling the Boer countries, but the nation which "rules the waves" exhausted every means to make the Boers' air-hole as small as possible by placing a number of warships outside the entrance of Delagoa Bay, and by establishing a blockade of the port of Lourenco Marques.

Lourenco Marques, in itself, was valueless to the Boers, for it had always been nothing more than a vampire feeding upon the Transvaal, but as an outlet to the sea and as a haven for foreign ships bearing men, arms, and encouragement it was invaluable. In the hands of the Boers Delagoa Bay would have been worse than useless, for the warships could have taken possession of it and sealed it tightly on the first day of the war, but as a Portuguese possession it was the only friend that the Boers were able to find during their long period of need. Without it, the Boers would have been unable to hold any intercourse with foreign countries, no envoys could have been despatched, no volunteers could have entered the country, and they would have been ignorant of the opinion of the world--a factor in the brave resistance against their enemy which was by no means infinitesimal. Delagoa Bay was the Boers' one window through which they could look at the world, and through which the world could watch the brave struggle of the farmer-citizens of the veld-republics.

The Portuguese authorities at Delagoa Bay long ago established a reputation for adroitness in extracting revenues whenever and wherever it was possible to find a stranger within their gates, but the war afforded them such excellent opportunities as they had never enjoyed before. Being the gate of the Boer country was a humanitarian privilege, but it also was a remunerative business, and never since Vasco de Gama discovered the port were so many choice facilities afforded for increasing the revenue of the colony. Nor was the Latin's mind wanting in concocting schemes for filling the Portuguese coffers when the laws were lax on the subject, for it was the simplest arrangement to frame a regulation suitable for every new condition that arose. The Portuguese were willing to be the medium between the Boers and the people of other parts of the earth, but they asked for and received a large percentage of the profits.

When the mines of the Johannesburg gold district were closed down, and the Portuguese heard that they would no longer receive a compulsory contribution of four shillings from every native who crossed the border to work in the mines, the officials felt uneasy on account of the great decrease in the amount of public revenues, but it did not worry them for any great length of time. They met the situation by imposing a tax of eight shillings upon every one of the thousands of natives who returned from the mines to their homes in Portuguese territory. About the same time the Uitlanders from the Transvaal reached Lourenco Marques, and, in order to calm the Portuguese mind, every one of the thousands of men and women who took part in that exodus was compelled to pay a transit tax, ranging from eight shillings to a sovereign, according to the size of the tip tendered to the official.

When the van of the foreign volunteers reached the port there was a new situation to be dealt with, and again the principle of "When in doubt impose a tax" was satisfactorily employed. Men who had just arrived in steamers, and who had never seen Portuguese territory, were obliged to secure a certificate, indicating that they had not been inhabitants of the local jail during the preceding six months; a certificate from the consular representative of their country, showing that they possessed good characters; another from the Governor-General to show that they did not purpose going into the Transvaal to carry arms; a fourth from the local Transvaal consul to indicate that he held no objections to the traveller's desire to enter the Boer country; and one or two other passports equally weighty in their bearing on the subject were necessary before a person was able to leave the town. Each one of these certificates was to be secured only upon the payment of a certain number of thousand reis and at an additional expenditure of time and nervous energy, for none of the officials could speak a word of any language except Portuguese, and all the applicants were men of other nationalities and tongues. The expenditure in connection with the certificates was more than a sovereign for every person, and as there were thousands of travellers into the Boer countries while the war continued the revenues of the Government were correspondingly great. To crown it all, the Portuguese imposed the same tax upon all travellers who came into the country from the Transvaal with the intention of sailing to other ports. The Government could not be charged with favouritism in the matter of taxation, for every man, woman, and child who stepped on Portuguese soil was similarly treated. There was no charge for entering the country, but the jail yawned for him who refused to pay when leaving it.

Not unlike the patriots in Cape Town and Durban, the hotel and shopkeepers of Lourenco Marques took advantage of the presence of many strangers and made extraordinary efforts to secure the residue of the money which did not fall into the coffers of the Government. At the Cardoza Hotel, the only establishment worthy of the name, a tax of a sovereign was levied for sleeping on a bare floor; drivers of street cabs scorned any amount less than a golden sovereign for carrying one passenger to the consulates; lemonades were two shillings each at the kiosks; and physicians charged three pounds a call when travellers remained in the town several days and contracted the deadly coast-fever. At the Custom House duties of ten shillings were levied upon foreign flags, unless the officer was liberally tipped, in which event it was not necessary to open the luggage. It was a veritable harvest for every one who chose to take advantage of the opportunities offered, and there were but few who did not make the foreigners their victims.

The blockade by the British warships placed a premium upon dishonesty, and of those who gained most by it the majority were British subjects. The vessels which succeeded in passing the blockading warships were invariably consigned to Englishmen, and without exception these were unpatriotic enough to sell the supplies to agents employed by the Transvaal Government. Just as Britons sold guns and ammunition to the Boers before the war, these men of the same nation made exorbitant profits on supplies which were necessary to the burgher army. Lourenco Marques was filled with men who were taking advantage of the state of affairs to grow wealthy by means which were not legitimate, and the leaders in almost every enterprise of that nature were British subjects, although there were not a few Germans, Americans, and Frenchmen who succeeded in making the fortunes they deserved for remaining in such a horrible pest-hole as Lourenco Marques.

The railroad from Lourenco Marques to Ressana Garcia, at the Transvaal border, was interesting only from the fact that it was more historical than comfortable for travelling purposes. As the train passed through the dry, dusty, and uninteresting country, which was even too poor and unhealthy for the blacks, the mind speculated upon the proposition whether the Swiss judges who decided the litigation concerning the road would have spent ten years in making a decision if they had been compelled to conduct their deliberation within sight of the railway. The land adjoining the railroad was level, well timbered and well watered, and the vast tracts of fine grass give the impression that it might be an excellent country for farming, but it was in the belt known as the fever district, and white men avoided it as they would a cholera-infested city. Shortly before the train arrived at the English river several lofty white-stone pyramids on either side of the railway were passed, and the Transvaal was reached. A long iron bridge spanning the river was crossed, and the train reached the first station in the Boer country, Komatipoort.

Courteous Boer officials entered the train and requested the passengers to disembark with all their luggage, for the purpose of custom-examination. No gratuities were accepted there, as at Lourenco Marques, and nothing escaped the vigilance of the bearded inspectors. Trunks and luggage were carefully scrutinised, letters read line by line and word for word; revolvers and ammunition promptly confiscated if not declared; and even the clothing of the passengers was faithfully examined. Passports were closely investigated, and, when all appeared to be thoroughly satisfactory, a white cross was chalked on the boots of the passengers, and they were free to proceed farther inland. The field-cornet of the district was one of the few Boers at the station, and he performed the duties of his office by introducing himself to certain passengers whom he believed to be foreign volunteers, and offering them gratuitous railway tickets to Pretoria. No effort was made to conceal the fact that the volunteers were welcome in the country, and nothing was left undone to make the foreigners realise that their presence was appreciated.

After Komatipoort was passed the train crept slowly into the mountainous district, where huge peaks pierced the clouds and gigantic boulders overhung the tracks. Narrow defiles stretched away in all directions and the sounds of cataracts in the Crocodile River flowing alongside the iron path drowned the roar of the train. Flowering, vari-coloured plants, huge cacti, and thick tropical vegetation lined the banks of the river, and occasionally the thatched roof of a negro's hut peered out over the undergrowth, to indicate that a few human beings chose that wild region for their abode. Hour after hour the train crept along narrow ledges up the mountains' sides, then dashed down declines and out upon small level plains which, with their surrounding and towering eminences, had the appearance of vast green bowls. In that impregnable region lay the small town of Machadodorp, which, later, became the capital of the Transvaal. A few houses of corrugated iron, a pretty railway-station, and much scenery, serves as a worthy description of the town at the junction of the purposed railway to the gold-fields of Lydenburg.

After a journey of twelve hours through the fever country the train reached the western limit of that belt and rested for the night in a small, green, cup-shaped valley bearing the descriptive name of Waterval Onder--"under the waterfall." The weary passengers found more corrugated iron buildings and the best hotel in South Africa. The host, Monsieur Mathis, a French Boer, and his excellent establishment came as a breath of fresh air to a stifling traveller on the desert, and long will they live in the memories of the thousands of persons who journeyed over the railroad during the war. After the monotonous fare of an east-coast steamer and the mythical meals of a Lourenco Marques hotel, the roast venison, the fresh milk and eggs of Mathis were as welcome as the odour of the roses that filled the valley.

The beginning of the second day's journey was characterised by a ride up and along the sides of a magnificent gorge through which the waters of the Crocodile River rushed from the lofty plateau of the high veld to the wildernesses of the fever country and filled that miniature South African Switzerland with myriads of rainbows. A long, curved, and inclined tunnel near the top of the mountain led to the undulating plains of the Transvaal--a marvellously rapid transition from a region filled with nature's wildest panoramas to one that contained not even a tree or rock or cliff to relieve the monotony of the landscape. On the one side of this natural boundary line was an immense territory every square mile of which contained mountain passes which a handful of Boers could hold against an invading army; on the other side there was hardly a rock behind which a burgher rifleman could conceal himself. Here herds of cattle and flocks of sheep, instead of wild beasts, sped away from the roar of the train; here there was the daub and wattle cottage of the farmer instead of the thatched hut of the native savage.

Small towns of corrugated iron and mud-brick homes and shops appeared at long intervals on the veld; grass-fires displayed the presence of the Boer farmer with his herds, and the long ox-teams slowly rolling over the plain signified that not all the peaceful pursuits of a small people at war with a great nation had been abandoned. The coal-mines at Belfast, with their towering stacks and clouds of smoke, gave the first evidence of the country's wondrous underground wealth, and then farther on in the journey came the small city of Middleburg with its slate-coloured corrugated iron roofs in marked contrast to the green veld grass surrounding it. There appeared armed and bandoliered Boers, prepared to join their countrymen in the field, with wounded friends and sad-faced women to bid farewell to them. While the train lay waiting at the station small commandos of burghers came dashing through the dusty streets, bustled their horses into trucks at the rear end of the passenger train, and in a few moments they were mingling with the foreign volunteers in the coaches. Grey-haired Boers gravely bade adieu to their wives and children, lovers embraced their weeping sweethearts, and the train moved on toward Pretoria and the battlefields where these men were to risk their lives for the life of their country.

Historic ground, where Briton and Boer had fought before, came in view. Bronkhorst Spruit, where a British commander led more than one hundred of his men to death in 1880, lay to the left of the road in a little wooded ravine. Farther on toward Pretoria appeared rocky kopjes, where afterwards the Boers, retreating from the capital city, gathered their disheartened forces, and resisted the advance of the enemy. Eerste Fabriken was a hamlet hardly large enough to make an impression upon the memory, but it marked a battlefield where the burghers fought desperately. Children were then gathering peaches from the trees, whose roots drank the blood of heroes months afterwards. Several miles farther on were the hills on the outskirts of Pretoria, where, in the war of 1881, the Boer laagers sent forth men to encompass the city and to prevent the British besieged in it from escaping. It was ground hallowed in Boer history since the early voortrek-kers crossed the ridges of the Magaliesburg and sought protection from the savage hordes of Moselekatse in the fertile valley of the Aapjes River.

Pretoria in war-time was most peaceful. In the days before the commence-ment of hostilities it was a city of peace as contrasted with the metropolis, Johannesburg, and its warring citizens, but when cannon were roaring on the frontier, Pretoria itself seemed to escape even the echoes. After the first com-mandos had departed the city streets were deserted, and only women and children gathered at the bulletin boards to learn the fate of the burgher armies.

The stoeps of houses and cottages were deserted of the bearded yeomanry, and the halls of the Government buildings resounded only with the tread of those who were not old or strong enough to bear arms. The long ox-wagons which in former times were so common in the streets were not so frequently to be seen, but whenever one of them rolled toward the market square, it was a Boer woman who cracked the raw-hide whip over the heads of the oxen. Pretoria was the same quaint city as of old, but it lacked the men who were its most distinguishing feature. The black-garbed Volksraad members, the officials, and the old retired farmers, who were wont to discuss politics on the stoeps of the capitol and the Transvaal Hotel were absent. Inquiries concerning them could be addressed only to women and children, and the replies invariably were: "They are on commando," or, "They were killed in battle."

The scenes of activity in the city were few in number, and they were chiefly in connection with the arrival of foreign volunteers and the transit of burgher commandos on the way to the field. The Grand Hotel and the Transvaal Hotel, the latter of which was conducted by the Government for the temporary entertainment of the volunteers, were constantly filled with throngs of foreigners, comprising soldiers of fortune, Red Cross delegations, visitors, correspondents, and contractors, and almost every language except that of the Boers could be heard in the corridors. Occasionally a Boer burgher on leave of absence from the front appeared at the hotels for a respite from army rations, or to attend the funeral of a comrade in arms, but the foreigners were always predominant. Across the street, in the War Department, there were busy scenes when the volunteers applied for their equipments, and frequently there were stormy actions when the European tastes of the men were offended by the equipment offered by the Department officials. Men who desired swords and artistic paraphernalia for themselves and their horses felt slighted when the scant but serviceable equipment of a Boer burgher was offered to them, but sulking could not remedy the matter, and usually they were content to accept whatever was given to them. Former officers in European armies, noblemen and even professional men were constantly arriving in the city, and all seemed to be of the same opinion that commissions in the Boer army could be had for the asking. Some of these had their minds disabused with good grace, and went to the field as common burghers; others sulked for several weeks, but finally joined a commando, and a few returned to their homes without having heard the report of a gun. For those who chose to remain behind and enjoy the peacefulness of Pretoria, there was always enough of novelty and excitement among the foreigners to compensate partly for missing the events in the field.

The army contractors make their presence felt in all countries which are engaged in war, and Pretoria was filled with them. They were in the railway trains running to and from Lourenco Marques; in the hotel corridors, in all the Government departments, and everywhere in the city. A few of the naturalised Boers, who were most denunciatory of the British before the war and urged their fellow-countrymen to resort to arms, succeeded in evading the call to the field and were most energetic in supplying bread and supplies to the Government. Nor was their patriotism dimmed by many reverses of the army, and they selfishly demanded that the war should be continued indefinitely. Europeans and Americans who partook of the protection of the Government in times of peace, were transformed by war into grasping, insinuating contractors who revelled in the country's misfortune. Englishmen, unworthy of the name, enriched themselves by furnishing sinews of war to their country's enemy, and in order to secure greater wealth sought to prolong the war by cheering disheartened Boers and expressing faith in their final success. The chambers of the Government building were filled with men who had horses, wagons, flour, forage and clothing to offer at exorbitant prices, and in thousands of instances the embarrassed Government was obliged to pay whatever sums were demanded. Hand-in-hand with the contractors were the speculators who were taking advantage of the absence of the leading officials to secure valuable concessions, mining claims, and even gold mines. Before the war, when hordes of speculators and concession-seekers thronged the city, the scene was pathetic enough, but when all shrewd Raad members were at the front and unable to guard their country's interests the picture was dark and pitiful.

Pretoria seemed to have but one mood during the war. It was never deeply despondent nor gay. There was a sort of funereal atmosphere throughout the city, whether its residents were rejoicing over a Spion Kop or suffering from the dejection of a Paardeberg. It was the same grim throng of old men, women, and children who watched the processions of prisoners of war and attended the funerals at the quaint little Dutch church in the centre of the city. The finest victories of the army never changed the appearance of the city nor the mood of its inhabitants. There were no parades nor shouting when a victory was announced, and there was the same stoical indifference when the news of a bitter defeat was received. A victory was celebrated in the Dutch church by the singing of psalms, and a defeat by the offering of prayers for the success of the army.

The thousands of British subjects who were allowed to remain in the Transvaal, being of a less phlegmatic race, were not so calm when a victory of their nation's army was announced, and when the news of Cronje's surrender reached them they celebrated the event with almost as much gusto as if they had not been in the enemy's country. A fancy dress ball was held in Johannesburg in honour of the event, and a champagne dinner was given within a few yards of the Government buildings in Pretoria, but a few days later all the celebrants were transported across the border by order of the Government.

One of the pathetic features of Pretoria was the Boers' expression of faith in foreign mediation or intervention. At the outset of hostilities it seemed unreasonable that any European nation or America would risk a war with Great Britain for the purpose of assisting the Boers, yet there was hardly one burgher who did not cling steadfastly to the opinion that the war would be ended in such a manner. The idea had evidently been rooted in their mind that Russia would take advantage of Great Britain's entanglement in South Africa to occupy Herat and Northern India, and when a newspaper item to that effect appeared it was gravely presumed to indicate the beginning of the end. Some over-zealous Irishmen assured the Boers that, in the event of a South African war, their fellow-countrymen in the United States would invade Canada and involve Great Britain in an imbroglio over the Atlantic in order to save British America. For a few weeks the chimera buoyed up the Boers, but when nothing more than an occasional newspaper rumour was heard concerning it the rising in Ashanti was then looked upon as being the hoped-for boon. The departure of the three delegates to Europe and America was an encouraging sign to them, and it was firmly believed that they would be able to induce France, Russia, or America to offer mediation or intervention. The two Boer newspapers, the Pretoria Volksstem and the Johannesburg *Standard and Diggers' News*, dwelt at length upon every favourable token of foreign assistance, however trifling, and attempted to strengthen hopes which at hardly any time seemed capable of realisation. It was not until after the war had been in progress for more than six months that the Boers saw the futility of placing faith in foreign aid, and afterwards they fought like stronger men.

The consuls who represented the foreign Governments at Pretoria, and through whom the Boers made representations for peace, were an exceptionally able body of men, and their duties were as varied as they were arduous. The French and German consuls were busied with the care of the vast mining interests of their countrymen, besides the partial guardianship of the hundreds of French and German volunteers in the Boer army. They were called upon to entertain noblemen as well as bankrupts; to bandage wounds and to bury the dead; to find lost relatives and to care for widows and orphans. In times of peace the duties of a consul in Pretoria were not light, but during hostilities they were tenfold heavier. To the American consul, Adelbert S. Hay, and his associate, John G. Coolidge, fell more work than to all the others combined. Besides caring for the American interests in the country, Consul Hay was charged with the guardianship of the six thousand British prisoners of war in the city as well as with the care of the financial interests of British citizens. Every one of the thousands of letters to and from the prisoners was examined in the American Consulate so that they might carry with them no breach of neutrality; almost twenty thousand pounds, as well as tons of luxuries, were distributed by him to the prisoners; while the letters and cablegrams concerning the health and where-abouts of soldiers which reached him every week were far in excess of the number of communications which arrived at the Consulate in a year of peaceful times. Consul Hay was in good favour with the Boer Government notwithstand-ing his earnest efforts to perform his duties with regard to the British prisoners and interests, and of the many consuls who have represented the United States in South Africa none performed his duties more intelligently or with more credit to his country.

One of the most interesting and important events in Pretoria before the Brit-ish occupation of the city was the meeting of the Volksraads on May 7th. It was a gathering of the warriors who survived the war which they themselves had brought about seven months before, and, although the enemy to whom they had thrown down the gauntlet was at their gates, they were as resolute and deter-mined as on that October day when they voted to pit the Boer farmer against the British lion. The seats of many of those who took part in that memorable meeting were filled with palms and evergreens to mark the patriots' deaths, but the vierkleur and the cause remained to spur the living. Generals, commandants, and burghers, no longer in the grimy costumes of the battlefield, but in the black garb of the legislator, filled the circles of chairs; bandoliered burghers, consuls and military attachés in spectacular uniform, business men, and women with tear-stained cheeks filled the auditorium; while on the official benches were the heads of departments and the Executive Council, State Secretary Reitz and General Schalk Burger. The Chairman of the Raad, General Lucas Meyer, fresh from the battlefield, attracted the attention of the throng by announcing the arrival of the President. Spectators, Raad members, officials, all rose to their feet, and Paul Kruger, the Lion of Rustenburg, the Afrikander captain, entered the Chamber and occupied a seat of honour.

GENERAL LUCAS J. MEYER

Grave affairs occupied the attention of the country and there were many pressing matters to be adjusted, was the burden of the meeting, but the most important work was the defence of the country, and all the members were as a unit that their proper places were to be found with the burghers in the field. There was no talk of ending the war, or of surrender; the President leading in the proposition to continue hostilities until a conclusion successful to the Boer cause was attained. "Shall we lose courage?" he demanded. "Never! Never!! Never!!!" and then added reverently: "May the people and the officers, animated and inspired by a Higher Power, realising their duty, not only to those brave ones who have already sacrificed their lives for their Fatherland, but also to posterity that expects a free country, continue and persevere in this war to the end." With these words of their aged chieftain engraved on their hearts to strengthen their resolution the members of the Volksraads doffed the garb of legislators and returned to their commandos to inspire them with new zeal and determination.

After that memorable meeting of the Volksraads Pretoria again assumed the appearance of a city of peace, but the rapid approach of the forces of the enemy soon transformed it into a scene of desperation and panic. Men with drawn faces dashed through the city to assist their hard-pressed countrymen in the field; tearful women with children on their arms filled the churches with their moans and prayers; deserters fleeing homeward exaggerated fresh disasters and increased the tension of the populace--tears and terror prevailed almost everywhere. Railway stations were filled with throngs intent on escaping from the coming disaster, commandos of breathless and blood-stained burghers entered the city, and soon the voice of the conquerors' cannon reverberated among the hills and valleys of the capital. Above the noise and din of the threatened city rose the calm assurance of Paul Kruger: "Have good cheer, God will be with our people in the end."

2. From Farm to Battlefield

In the olden days, before men with strange languages and customs entered their country and disturbed the serenity of their life, the Boers were accustomed to make annual trips to the north in search of game, and to exterminate the lions which periodically attacked their flocks and herds. It was customary for relatives to form parties, and these trekked with their long ox-wagons far into the northern Transvaal, and oftentimes into the wilderness beyond the Zambesi. Women and children accompanied the expeditions and remained behind in the ox-wagons while the men rode away into the bush to search for buck, giraffe, and lion. Hardy men and women these were who braved the dangers of wild beasts and the terrors of the fever country, yet these treks to the north were as certain annual functions as the Nachtmaals in the churches. Men who went into the wild bush to hunt for the lions, which had been their only unconquerable enemy for years, learned to know no fear, and with their wives and children formed as hardy a race as virgin soil ever produced. With these pioneers it was not a matter of great pride to have shot a lion, but it was considered a disgrace to have missed one. To husband their sparse supplies of ammunition was their chief object, and to waste a shot by missing the target was to become the subject of good-natured derision and ridicule. Fathers, sons, and grandsons entered the bush together, and when there was a lion or other wild beast to be stalked the amateur hunter was initiated into the mysteries of backwoodsmanship by his experienced elders. Consequently the Boers became a nation of proficient lion-hunters, and efficiently ridded their country of the pest which continually threatened their safety, the safety of their families and that of their possessions of live-stock.

In later years, when the foreigner who bought his farms and searched for the wealth hidden on them became so numerous that the Boer appeared to be an unwelcome guest in his own house, the old-time lion-hunter had foundation for believing that a new enemy had suddenly arisen. The Boer attempted to placate the new enemy by means which failed. Afterward a bold but unsuccessful inroad was made into the country for the purpose of relieving him of the necessity of ruling it. Thereupon the old-time lion-fighting spirit arose within the Boer, and he began to prepare for future hunting expeditions. He stocked his arsenals with the best guns and ammunition the world produced, and he secured instructors to teach him the most modern and approved methods of fighting the new-style lion. He erected forts and stockades in which he might take refuge in the event that the lions should prove too strong and numerous, and he made laws and regulations so that there might be no delay when the proper moment arrived for attacking the enemy. While these matters were being perfected further efforts were made to conciliate the enemy, but they proved futile, and it became evident that the farmer and the lion of 1899 were as implacable enemies as the farmer and lion of 1850. The lion of 1899 believed his cause to be as just as did the lion of half a century before, while the farmer felt that the lion, having been created by Nature, had a just claim upon Nature and her works for support, but desired that sustenance should be sought from other parts of Nature's stores. He insisted, moreover, if the lion wished to remain on the plantation that he should not question the farmer's ownership nor assume that the lion was an animal of a higher and finer grade than the farmer.

A meeting between the representatives of the lions and the farmers led to no better understanding; in fact when, several days afterward, all the farmers gathered at the historic Paardekraal monument, they were unanimously of the opinion that the lion should be driven out of the country, or at least subdued to such an extent that peace might come and remain. Not since the days of 1877, when, at the same spot, each Boer, holding a stone above his head, vowed to shed his last drop of blood in defence of his country, was the community of farmers so indignant and excited. The aged President himself, fresh from the conference with the lions, urged his countrymen to prevent a conflict but to fight valiantly for their independence and rights if the necessity arose. Piet Joubert, who bore marks of a former conflict with the enemy, wept as he narrated the efforts which had been made to pacify the lions, and finally expressed the belief that every farmer in the country would yield his life's blood rather than surrender the rights for which their fathers had bled and died. When other leaders had spoken, the picturesque custom of renewing the oath of fealty to the country's flag was observed, as it had been every fifth year since the days of Majuba Hill. Ten thousand farmers uncovered their heads, raised their eyes toward the sky and repeated the Boer oath:--

"In the presence of God Almighty, who searcheth the hearts of men, from our homes in the Transvaal we have journeyed to meet again, Free burghers, we ask His mercy and trust in His grace and bind ourselves and our children in a solemn oath to be faithful to one another and to stand by one another in repelling our enemy with our last drop of life-blood. So truly help us, God Almighty."

Ten thousand voices then joined in singing the national anthem and a psalm, and the memorable meeting at this fount of patriotism was closed with a prayer and a benediction.

After this meeting it was uncertain for some months which should attack first; both were preparing as rapidly as possible for the conflict, and the advantage seemed to lie with the one who would strike first. The leaders of the lions seemed to have forgotten that they had lion-hunters as their opponents, and the farmers neglected to take into account the fact that the lion tribe was exceedingly numerous and spread over the whole earth. When the leading farmers met in conclave at Pretoria and heard the demands of the lions they laughed at them, sent an ultimatum in reply, and started for the frontier to join those of their countrymen who had gone there days before to watch that no body of lions should make another surreptitious attack upon their country. Another community of farmers living to the south, who had also been harassed by the lions for many years and felt that their future safety lay in the subjugation of the lion tribe, joined their neighbours in arms and went forth with them to the greatest lion-hunt that South Africa has ever had.

The enemy and all other men called it war, but to the Boers it was merely a hunt for lions such as they had engaged in oftentimes before.

The old Boer farmer hardly needed the proclamation from Pretoria to tell him that there was to be a lion-hunt, and that he should prepare for it immediately. He had known that the hunt was inevitable long before October 11, 1899, and he had made preparations for it months and even years before. When the official notification from the Commandant-General reached him through the field-cornet of the district in which he lived, he was prepared in a few minutes to start for the frontier where the British lions were to be found. The new Mauser rifle, which the Government had given him a year or two before, was freshly oiled and its working order inspected. The bandolier, filled with bright new cartridges, was swung over his shoulder, and then, after putting a Testament into his coat pocket, he was ready to proceed. He despised a uniform of any kind as smacking of anti-republican ideas and likely to attract the attention of the enemy. The same corduroy or mole-skin trousers, dark coat, wide-brimmed hat, and home-made shoes which he was accustomed to wear in every-day life on the farm were good enough for a hunting expedition, and he needed and yearned for nothing better. A uniform would have caused him to feel uneasy and out of place, and when lions were the game he wanted to be thoroughly comfortable so that his arm and aim might be steady. His vrouw, who was filling a linen sack with bread, biltong, and coffee to be consumed on his journey to the hunting grounds, may have taken the opportunity while he was cleaning his rifle to sew a rosette of the vierkleur of the Republic on his hat, or, remembering the custom observed in the old-time wars against the natives, may have found the fluffy brown tail of a meerkat and fixed it on the upturned brim of his grimy hat. When these few preparations were concluded the Black servant brought his master's horse and fixed to the front of the saddle a small roll containing a blanket and a mackintosh. To another part of the saddle he strapped a small black kettle to be used for the preparation of the lion-hunter's only luxury, coffee, and then the list of impedimenta was complete. The horseman who brought the summons to go to the frontier had hardly reached the neighbouring farmhouse when the Boer lion-hunter, uniformed, outfitted, and armed, was on his horse's back and ready for any duty at any place. With a rifle, bandolier, and a horse the Boer felt as if he were among kindred spirits, and nothing more was necessary to complete his temporal happiness. The horse is a part of the Boer hunter, and he might as well have gone to the frontier without a rifle as to go in the capacity of a foot soldier. The Boer is the modern Centaur, and therein is found an explanation for part of his success in hunting.

When once the Boer left his home he became an army unto himself. He needed no one to care for himself and his horse, nor were the leaders of the army obliged to issue myriads of orders for his guidance. He had learned long before that he should meet the other hunters of his ward at a certain spot in case there was a call to arms, and thither he went as rapidly as his pony could carry him. When he arrived at the meeting-place he found all his neighbours and friends gathered in groups and discussing the situation. Certain ones of them had brought with them big white-tented ox-wagons for conveying ammunition, commissariat stores, and such extra luggage as some might wish to carry; and these were sent ahead as soon as the field-cornet, the military leader of the ward, learned that all his men had arrived from their homes. The individual hunters then formed what was called a commando, whether it consisted of fifteen or fifty men, and pro-ceeded in a body to a second pre-arranged meeting-place, where all the ward-commandos of a certain district were asked to congregate. When all these commandos had arrived in one locality, they fell under the authority of the commandant who had been elected to that post by the burghers at the preceding election. This official had received his orders directly from the Commandant-General, and but little time was consumed in disseminating them to the burghers through the various field-cornets. After all the ward-commandos had arrived, the district-commando was set in motion toward that part of the frontier where its services were required; and a most unwarlike spectacle it presented as it rolled along over the muddy, slippery veld. In the van were the huge, lumbering wagons with hordes of hullabalooing natives cracking their long raw-hide whips and urging the sleek, long-horned oxen forward through the mud. Following the wagon-train came the cavalcade of armed lion-hunters, grim and determined-looking enough from a distance, but most peaceful and inoffensive when once they understood the stranger's motives. No order or discipline was visible in the commando on the march, and if the rifles and bandoliers had not appeared so prominently it might readily have been mistaken for a party of Nachtmaal celebrants on the way to Pretoria. Now and then some youths emerged from the crowd and indulged in an impromptu horse-race, only to return and receive a chiding from their elders for wasting their horses' strength unnecessarily. Occasionally the keen eyes of a rider spied a buck in the distance, and then several of the lion-hunters sped obliquely off the track and replenished the commando larder with much smaller game than was the object of their expedition.

If the commando came from a district far from the frontier, it proceeded to the railway station nearest to the central meeting-place, and then embarked for the front. No extraordinary preparations were necessary for the embarking of a large commando, nor was much time lost before the hunters were speeding towards their destination. Every man placed his own horse in a cattle-car, his saddle, bridle, and haversack in the passenger-coach, and then assisted in hoisting the cumbersome ox-wagons on flat-top trucks. There were no specially deputised men to entrain the horses, others to load the wagons, and still others to be subtracted from the fighting strength of the nation by attending to such detail duties as require the services of hundreds of men in other armies.

After the burghers were entrained and the long commando train was set in motion the most fatiguing part of the campaign was before them. To ride on a South African railway is a disagreeable duty in times of peace, but in war-times, when trains were long and overcrowded, and the rate of progress never higher than fifteen miles an hour, then all other campaigning duties were pleasurable enjoyments. The majority of burghers, unaccustomed to journeying in railway trains, relished the innovation and managed to make merry even though six of them, together with all their saddles and personal luggage, were crowded into one compartment. The singing of hymns occupied much of their time on the journey, and when they tired of this they played practical jokes upon one another and amused themselves by leaning out of the windows and jeering at the men who were guarding the railway bridges and culverts. At the stations they grasped their coffee-pots and rushed to the locomotive to secure hot water with which to prepare their beverage. It seldom happened that any Boer going to the front carried any liquor with him and, although the delays and vexations of the journey were sufficiently irritating to serve as an excuse, drunkenness practically never occurred. Genuine good-fellowship prevailed among them, and no quarrelling was to be observed. It seemed as if every one of them was striving to live the ideal life portrayed in the Testament which they read assiduously scores of times every day. Whether a train was delayed an hour at a siding or whether it stopped so suddenly that all were thrown from their seats, there was no profane language, but usually jesting and joking instead. Little discomforts which would cause an ordinary American or European soldier to use volumes of profanity were passed by without notice or comment by these psalm-singing Boers, and inconveniences of greater moment, like the disarrangement of the commissariat along the route, caused only slight remonstrances from them. An angry man was as rarely seen as one who cursed, and more rare than either was an intoxicated one.

Few of the men were given to boasting of the valour they would display in warfare or of their abilities in marksmanship. They had no battle-cry of revenge like "Remember the *Maine*! " or "Avenge Majuba!" except it was the motto: "For God, Country, and Independence!" which many bore on the bands of their hats and on the stocks of their rifles. Very occasionally one boasted of the superiority of the Boer, and still more rarely would one be heard to set three months as the limit required to conquer the British army. The name of Jameson, the raider, was frequently heard, but always in a manner which might have led one unacquainted with recent Transvaal history to believe that he was a patron-saint of the Republic. It was not a cry of "Remember Jameson" for the wrongs he committed but rather a plea to honour him for having placed the Republic on its guard against the dangers which they believed threatened it from beyond its borders. It was frequently suggested, when his name was mentioned, that after the war a monument should be erected to him because he had given them warning and that they had profited by the warning to the extent that they had armed themselves thoroughly. Seldom was any boasting concerning the number of the enemy that would fall to Boer bullets; instead there was a tone of sorrow when they spoke of the soldiers of the Queen who would die on the field of battle while fighting for a cause concerning the justice or injustice of which the British soldier could not speak.

After the commando-train reached its destination the burghers again took charge of their own horses and conveyances, and in even less time than it required to place them on the train they were unloaded and ready to proceed to the point where the generals needed their assistance. The Boer was always considerate of his horse, and it became a custom to delay for several hours after leaving the train, in order that the animals might feed and recover from the fatigues of the journey before starting out on a trek over the veld. After the horses had been given an opportunity to rest, the order to "upsaddle" came from the commandant, and then the procession, with the ox-wagons in the van, was again formed. The regular army order was then established, scouts were sent ahead to determine the location of the enemy, and the officers for the first time appeared to lead their men in concerted action against the opposing forces. To call the Boer force an army was to add unwarranted elasticity to the word, for it had but one quality in common with such armed forces as Americans or Europeans are accustomed to call by that name. The Boer army fought with guns and gunpowder, but it had no discipline, no drills, no forms, no standards, and not even a roll-call. It was an enlarged edition of the hunting parties which a quarter-century ago went into the Zoutpansberg in search of game--it was a massive aggregation of lion-hunters.

3. Composition of the Army

A visitor in one of the laagers in Natal once spoke of a Boer burgher as a "soldier." A Boer from the Wakkerstroom district interrupted his speech and said there were no Boer soldiers. "If you want us to understand concerning whom you are talking," he continued, "you must call us burghers or farmers. Only the English have soldiers." It was so with all the Boers; none understood the term soldier as applying to anybody except their enemy, while many considered it an insult to be called a soldier, as it implied, to a certain extent, that they were fighting for hire. In times of peace the citizen of the Boer republics was called a burgher, and when he took up arms and went to war he received no special title to distinguish him from the man who remained at home. "My burghers," Paul Kruger was wont to call them before the war, and when they came forth from battle they were content when he said, "My burghers are doing well." The Boers were proud of their citizenship, and when their country was in danger they went forth as private citizens and not as bold warriors to protect it.

There was a law in the two republics which made it incumbent upon all burghers between the ages of sixteen and sixty to join a commando and to go to war when it was necessary. There was no law, however, which prevented a man, of whatever youthfulness or age, to assist in the defence of his country, and in consequence the Boer commandos contained almost the entire male population between the ages of thirteen and eighty years. In peaceful times the Boer farmer rarely travelled away from his home unless he was accompanied by his family, and he would have felt the pangs of homesickness if he had not been continually surrounded by his wife and children. When the war began it was not an easy matter for the burgher to leave his home for an indefinite period, and in order that he might not be lonely he took with him all his sons who were strong enough to carry rifles. The Boer youth develops into manhood early in life in the mild South African climate, and the boy of twelve and thirteen years is the equal in physical development of the American or European youth of sixteen or seventeen. He was accustomed to live on the open veld and hunting with his elders, and, when he saw that all his former companions were going to war, he begged for permission to accompany the commando. The Boer boy of twelve does not wear knickerbocker trousers as the youth of like age in many other countries, but he is clothed exactly like his father, and, being almost as tall, his youthful appearance is not so noticeable when he is among a large number of his countrymen. Scores of boys not more than twelve years were in the laagers in Natal, and hundreds of less age than the minimum prescribed by the military law were in every commando in the country. When Ladysmith was still besieged one youth of eleven years was conspicuous in the Standerton laager. He seemed to be a mere child, yet he had the patriotism of ten men. He followed his father everywhere, whether into battle or to the spring for water.

"When my father is injured or killed, I will take his rifle," was his excuse for being away from home. When General De Wet captured seven cannon from the enemy at the battle of Sannaspost two of the volunteers to operate them were boys aged respectively fourteen and fifteen years. Pieter J. Henning, of the Potchefstroom commando, who was injured in the battle of Scholtznek on December 11th, was less than fifteen years old, yet his valour in battle was as conspicuous as that of any of the burghers who took part in the engagement. Teunis H.C. Mulder, of the Pretoria commando, celebrated his sixteenth birthday only a few days before he was twice wounded at Ladysmith on November 9th, and Willem François Joubert, a relative of the Commandant-General, was only fifteen years old when he was wounded at Ladysmith on October 30th. At the battle of Koedoesrand, fifteen-year-old Pieter de Jager, of the Bethlehem commando, was seriously injured by a shell while he was conveying his injured father from the field. With the army of General Cronje captured at Paardeberg were no less than a hundred burghers who had not reached the sixteenth year, and among those who escaped from the laager in the river-bed were two Bloemfontein boys named Roux, aged twelve and fourteen years.

BATTLEFIELD OF COLENSO, DECEMBER 15, 1899

1. *GENERAL LOUIS BOTHA'S COMMANDO*
2. *BOKSBURG COMMANDO*
3. *COLENSO*
4. *KRUGERSDORP COMMANDO*
5. *WAKKERSTROM COMMANDO*
6. *ERMELO COMMANDO*
7. *SWAZILAND POLICE*
8. *ERMELO COMMANDO*
9. *BRITISH CAMP, CHIEVELY*
10. *TUGELA RIVER*

At Colenso a Wakkerstroom youth of twelve years captured three English scouts and compelled them to march ahead of him to the commandant's tent. During one of the lulls in the fighting at Magersfontein a burgher of fifteen years crept up to within twenty yards of three British soldiers and shouted "Hands up!" Thinking that there were other Boers in the vicinity the men dropped their guns and became prisoners of the boy, who took them to General De la Rey's tent. When the General asked the boy how he secured the prisoners the lad replied, nonchalantly, "Oh, I surrounded them." These youths who accompanied the commando were known as the "Penkop Regiment"--a regiment composed of school children--and in their connection an amusing story has been current in the Boer country ever since the war of 1881, when large numbers of children less than fifteen years old went with their fathers to battle. The story is that after the fight at Majuba Hill, while the peace negotiations were in progress, Sir Evelyn Wood, the Commander of the British forces, asked General Joubert to see the famous Penkop Regiment. The Boer General gave an order that the regiment should be drawn up in a line before his tent, and when this had been done General Joubert led General Wood into the open and introduced him to the corps. Sir Evelyn was sceptical for some time, and imagined that General Joubert was joking, but when it was explained to him that the youths really were the much-vaunted Penkop Regiment he advised them to return to their school-books.

When a man has reached the age of sixty it may be assumed that he has out-lived his usefulness as a soldier; but not so with the Boer. There was not one man, but hundreds, who had passed the Biblical threescore years and ten but were fighting valiantly in defence of their country. Grey-haired men who, in another country, might be expected to be found at their homes reading the accounts of their grandsons' deeds in the war, went out on scouting duty and scaled hills with almost as much alacrity as the burghers only half their age. Men who could boast of being grandfathers were innumerable, and in almost any laager there could be seen father, sons, and grandsons, all fighting with equal vigour and enthusiasm. Paul Kruger is seventy-five years old, but there were many of his burghers several years older than he who went to the frontier with their commandos and remained there for several months at a time. A great-grandfather serving in the capacity of a private soldier, may appear like a mythical tale, but there were several such. Old Jan van der Westhuizen, of the Middelburg laager, was active and enthusiastic at eighty-two years, and felt more than proud of four great-grand-children. Piet Kruger, a relative of the President, and four years his senior, was an active participant in every battle in which the Rustenburg commando was engaged while it was in Natal, and he never once referred to the fact that he fought in the 1881 war and in the attack upon Jameson's men. Four of Kruger's sons shared the same tent and fare with him, and ten of his grandsons were burghers in different commandos. Jan C. van Tonder, of Boshof, exceeded the maximum of the military age by eight years, but he was early in the field, and was seriously wounded at the battle of Scholtznek on December 11th. General Joubert himself was almost seventy years old but as far as physical activity was concerned there were a score of burghers in his commando, each from five to ten years older, who exhibited more energy in one battle than he did during the entire Natal campaign. The hundreds of bridges and culverts along the railway lines in the Transvaal, the Orange Free State, and Upper Natal were guarded day and night by Boers more than sixty years old, who had volunteered to do the work in order that younger men might be sent to localities where their services might be more necessary. Other old Boers and cripples attended to the commissariat arrangements along the railways, conducted commissariat wagons, gathered forage for the horses at the front, and arranged the thousands of details which are necessary to the well-being and comfort of every army, however simple its organisation.

Among the Boers were many burghers who had assisted Great Britain in her former wars in South Africa--men who had fought under the British flag, but were now fighting against it. Colonel Ignace Ferreira, a member of one of the oldest Boer families, fought under Lord Wolseley in the Zulu war, and had the Order of the Commander of the Bath conferred upon him by the Queen. Colonel Ferreira was at the head of a commando at Mafeking. Paul Dietzch, the military secretary of General Meyer, fought under the British flag in the Gaika and several other native wars.

It was not only the extremely old and the extremely young who went to war; it was a transfer of the entire population of the two Republics to the frontiers, and no condition or position was sufficient excuse to remain behind. The professional man of Pretoria and Johannesburg was in a laager which was adjacent to a laager of farthest-back veld-farmers. Lawyers and physicians, photographers and grocers, speculators and sextons, judges and schoolmasters, schoolboys and barkeepers--all who were burghers locked their desks and offices and journeyed to the front. Even clergymen closed their houses of worship in the towns and remained among the commandos to pray and preach for those who did the fighting. The members of the Volksraads, who brought on the war by their ultimatum, were among the first in the field, and foremost in attacking the soldiers of their enemy. Students in European universities, who hastened home when war-clouds were gathering, went shoulder to shoulder into battle with the backwoodsman, the Boer takhaar. There was no pride among them; no class distinction which prevented a farmer from speaking to a millionaire. A graduate of Cambridge had as his boon companion for five months a farmer who thought the earth a square, and imagined the United States to be a political division of Australia.

BOERS WATCHING THE FIGHT AT DUNDEE

The Boer who was bred in a city or town good-naturedly referred to his country cousin as a "takhaar"--a man with grizzly beard and unkempt hair. It was a good descriptive term, and the takhaar was not offended when it was applied to him. The takhaar was the modern type of the old voortrekker Boer who, almost a hundred years ago, trekked north from Cape Colony, and after overcoming thousands of difficulties settled in the present Boer country. He was a religious, big-hearted countryman of the kind who would suspect a stranger until he proved himself worthy of trust. After that period was passed the takhaar would walk the veld in order that you might ride his horse. If he could not speak your language he would repeat a dozen times such words as he knew, meanwhile offering to you coffee, mutton, bread, and all the best that his laager larder afforded. He offered to exchange a pipe-load of tobacco with you, and when that occurred you could take it for granted that he was your friend for life. The takhaar was the man who went to the frontiers on his own responsibility weeks before the ultimatum was sent, and watched day and night lest the enemy might trample a rod beyond the bounds. He was the man who stopped Jameson, who climbed Majuba, and who fought the natives. The takhaar was the Boer before gold brought restless-ness into the country, and he was proud of his title. The fighting ability of the takhaar is best illustrated by repeating an incident which occurred after the battle of Dundee when a large number of Hussars were captured. One of the Hussar officers asked for the name of the regiment he had been fighting against. A fun-loving Boer replied that the Boers had no regiments; that their men were divided into three brigades--the Afrikanders, the Boers, and the Takhaars--a distinction which carried with it but a slight difference. "The Afrikander brigade," the Boer explained, "is fighting now. They fight like demons. When they are killed, then the Boers take the field. The Boers fight about twice as well and hard as the Afrikanders. As soon as all the Boers are killed, then come the takhaars, and they would rather fight than eat." The officer remained silent for a moment, then sighed and said, "Well, if that is correct, then our job is bigger than I thought it was."

The ideal Boer is a man with a bearded face and a flowing moustache, and in order to appear idyllic almost every Boer burgher, who was not thus favoured before war was began, engaged in the peaceful process of growing a beard. Young men who, in times of peace, detested hirsute adornments of the face allowed their beards and moustaches to grow, and after a month or two it was almost impossible to find one burgher who was without a growth of hair on his face. The wearing of a beard was almost equal to a badge of Boer citizenship, and for the time being every Boer was a takhaar in appearance if not in fact. The adoption of beards was not so much fancy as it was a matter of discretion. The Boer was aware of the fact that few of the enemy wore beards, and so it was thought quite ingenious for all burghers to wear facial adornments of that kind in order that friend and foe might be distinguished more readily at a distance.

Notwithstanding their ability to fight when it is necessary, it is doubtful whether twenty per cent of the Boer burghers in the commandos would be accepted for service in any continental or American army. The rigid physical examinations of many of the armies would debar thousands from becoming regular soldiers. There were men in the Boer forces who had only one arm, some with only one leg, others with only one eye; some were almost totally blind, while others would have felt happy if they could have heard the reports of their rifles. Men who were suffering from various kinds of illnesses, and who should have been in a physician's care, were to be seen in every laager. Men who wore spectacles were numerous, while those who suffered from diseases which debar a man from a regular army were without number. The high percentage of men unfit for military duty was not due to the Boer's unhealthfulness, for he is as healthy as farmers are in other parts of the earth. Take the entire male population of any district in Europe and America and compare the individuals with the standard required by army rules, and the result will not differ greatly from the result of the Boer examination. If all the youths and old men, the sick and maimed, could have been eliminated from the Boer forces, eighty per cent, would probably have been found to be a low estimate of the number thus subtracted from the total force. It would have been heartrending to many a continental or American general to see the unmilitary appearance of the Boer burgher, and in what manner an army of children, great-grandfathers, invalids, and blind men, with a handful of good men to leaven it, could be of any service whatever would have been quite beyond his conception. It was such a mixed force that a Russian officer, who at the outset of the war entered the Transvaal to fight, became disgusted with its unmilitary appearance and returned to his own country.

The accoutrement of the Boer burgher was none the less incongruous than the physical appearance of the majority of them, although no expensive uniform and trappings could have been of more practical value. The men of the Pretoria and Johannesburg commandos had the unique honor of going to the war in uniforms specially made for the purpose, but there was no regulation or law which compelled them to wear certain kinds of clothing. When these commandos went to the frontier several days before the actual warfare had begun they were clothed in khaki-coloured cloth of almost the same description as that worn by the soldiers whom they intended to fight. These two commandos were composed of town-folk who had absorbed many of the customs and habits of the foreigners who were in the country, and they felt that it would be more warlike if they should wear uniforms made specially for camp and field. The old Boers of the towns and the takhaars looked askance at the youth of Pretoria and Johannesburg in their uniforms, and shook their heads at the innovation as smacking too much of an anti-republican spirit.

Like Cincinnatus, the majority of the old Boers went directly from their farms to the battlefields, and they wore the same clothing in the laagers as they used when shearing their sheep or herding their cattle. When they started for the frontier the Boer farmers arranged matters so that they might be comfortable while the campaign continued. Many, it is true, dashed away from home at the first call to arms and carried with them, besides a rifle and bandolier, nothing but a mackintosh, blanket, and haversack of food. The majority of them, however, were solicitous of their future comfort and loaded themselves down with all kinds of luggage. Some went to the frontier with the big, four-wheeled ox-wagons and in these they conveyed cooking utensils, trunks, boxes with food and flour, mattresses, and even stoves. The Rustenburg farmers were specially solicitous about their comfort, and those patriotic old takhaars practically moved their families and household furniture to the camps. Some of the burghers took two or three horses each in order that there might be no delay or annoyance in case of misfortune by death or accident, and frequently a burgher could be seen who had one horse for himself, another for his camp utensils and extra clothing, and a third and fourth for native servants who cooked his meals and watched the horses while they grazed.

Without his horse the Boer would be of little account as a fighting man, and those magnificent little ponies deserve almost as much credit for such success as attended the campaign as their riders. If some South African does not frame a eulogy of the little beasts it will not be because they do not deserve it. The horse was half the Centaur and quite the life of him. Small and wiry, he was able to jog along fifty and sixty miles a day for several days in succession, and when the occasion demanded it, he was able to attain a rate of speed that equalled that of the ordinary South African railway train which, however, makes no claims to lightning-like velocity. He bore all kinds of weather, was not liable to sickness except in one season of the year, and he was able to work two and even three days without more than a blade of grass. He was able to thrive on the grass of the veld, and when winter killed that product he needed but a few bundles of forage a day to keep him in good condition. He climbed rocky mountain-sides as readily as a buck, and never wandered from a path by darkest night. He drank and apparently relished the murky water of mud-pools and needed but little attention with the currycomb and brush. He was trained to obey the slightest turn of the reins, and a slight whistle brought him to a full stop. When his master left him and went forward into battle the Boer pony remained in the exact position where he was placed, and when perchance a shell or bullet ended his existence, then the Boer paid a tribute to the value of his dead servant by refusing to continue the fight and by beating a hasty retreat.

In the early part of the campaign in Natal the laagers were filled with ox-wagons, and, in the absence of tents which were sadly wanted during that season of heavy rains, they stood in great stead to the burghers. The rear half of the wagons were tented with an arched roof, as all the trek-wagons are, and under these shelters the burghers lived. Many of the burghers who left their ox-wagons at home took small, light, four-wheeled carriages, locally called spiders, or the huge two-wheelers or Cape-carts so serviceable and common throughout the country. These were readily transformed into tents, and made excellent sleeping accommodations by night and transport-wagons for the luggage when the commandos moved from one place to another. When a rapid march was contemplated all the heavy wagons were left behind in charge of native servants with which every burgher was provided.

It was quite in keeping with their other ideas of personal comfort for many Boer burghers to carry a coloured parasol or an umbrella to protect them from the rays of the sun, and it was not considered beneath their dignity to wear a woman's shawl around their shoulders or head when the morning air was chilly. At first sight of these unique spectacles the stranger in the Boer country felt amused, but if he cared to smile at every unmilitary scene he would have had little time for other things. It was a republican army composed of republicans, and anything that smacked of the opposite was abhorred. There were no flags or insignia of any kind to lead the burghers on. What mottoes there were that expressed their cause were embroidered on the bands of their slouch-hats and cut on the stocks of their rifles. "For God and Freedom," "For Freedom, Land, and People," and "For God, Country, and Justice," were among the sentiments which some of the burghers carried into battle on their hats and rifles. Others had vierkleur ribbons as bands for their hats, while many carried on the upturned brim of their hats miniatures containing the photographs of the Presidents.

Aside from the dangers arising from a contact with the enemy and the heart-burns resulting from a long absence from his home, the Boer burgher's experiences at the front were not arduous. First and foremost he had a horse and rifle, and with these he was always more or less happy. He had fresh meat provided to him daily, and he had native servants to prepare and serve his meals for him. He was under no discipline whatever, and he could be his own master at all times. He generally had his sons or brothers with him in the same laager, and to a Boer there was always much joy in this. He could go on picket duty and have a brush with the enemy whenever he felt inclined to do so, or he could remain in his laager and never have a glimpse of the enemy. Every two months he was entitled to a ten days' leave of absence to visit his home, and at other times during the first five months of the war, his wife and children were allowed to visit him in his laager. If he was stationed along the northern or western frontiers of the Transvaal he was in the game country, and he was able to go on buck-shooting expeditions as frequently as he cared. He was not compelled to rise at a certain hour in the morning, and he could go to bed whenever he wished. There was no drill, no roll-calls, nor any of the thousands of petty details which the soldiers of even the Portuguese army are compelled to perform. As a result of a special law there was no work on Sundays or Church-holidays unless the enemy brought it about, and then, if he was a stickler for the observance of the Sabbath, he was not compelled to move a muscle. The Boer burgher could eat, sleep, or fight whenever he wished, and inasmuch as he was a law unto himself, there was no one who could compel him to change his habits. It was an ideal idle-man's mode of living and the foreign volunteers who had leaves of absence from their own armies made the most of their holiday, but in that respect they did not surpass their companion, the Boer burgher.

The most conspicuous feature of the Boer forces was the equality of the officers and the men, and the entire absence of any assumption of superiority by the leaders of the burghers. None of the generals or commandants wore any uniform of a distinctive type, and it was one of the most difficult problems to distinguish an officer from the burghers. All the officers, from the Commandant-General down to the corporal, carried rifles and bandoliers, and all wore the ordinary garb of a civilian, so that there was nothing to indicate the man's military standing. The officers associated with their men every hour of the day, and, in most instances, were able to call the majority of them by their Christian names. With one or two exceptions, all the generals were farmers before the war started, and consequently they were unable to assume any great degree of superiority over their farmer-burghers if they had wished to do so. General Meyer pitched quoits with his men, General Botha swapped tobacco with any one of his burghers, and General Smuts and one of his officers held the whist championship of their laager. Rarely a burgher touched his hat before speaking to an officer, but he invariably shook hands with him at meeting and parting. It is a Boer custom to shake hands with friends or strangers, and whenever a general visited a laager adjoining his own, the hand-shaking reminded one of the President's public reception days at Washington. When General Joubert went from camp to camp he greeted all the burghers who came near him with a grasp of the hand, and it was the same with all the other generals and officers. Whenever Presidents Kruger and Steyn went to the commandos, they held out their right hands to all the burghers who approached them, and one might have imagined that every Boer was personally acquainted with every other one in the republics. It was the same with strangers who visited the laagers, and many a sore wrist testified to the Boer's republicanism. Some one called it the "hand-shaking army," and it was a most descriptive title. Many of the burghers could not restrain from exercising their habit, and shook hands with British prisoners, much to the astonishment of the captured.

Another striking feature of life in the Boer laagers was the deep religious feeling which manifested itself in a thousand different ways. It is an easy matter for an irreligious person to scoff at men who pass through a campaign with prayer and hymn-singing, and it is just as easy to laugh at the man who reads his Testament at intervals of shooting at the enemy. The Boer was a religious man always, and when he went to war he placed as much faith in prayer and in his Testament as in his rifle. He believed that his cause was just, and that the Lord would favour those fighting for a righteous cause in a righteous spirit. On

October 11th, before the burghers crossed the frontier at Laing's Nek, a religious service was conducted. Every burgher in the commandos knelt on the ground and uttered a prayer for the success and the speedy ending of the campaign. Hymns were sung, and for a full hour the hills, whereon almost twenty years before many of the same burghers sang and prayed after the victory at Majuba, were resounding with the religious and patriotic songs of men going forward to kill and to be killed. In their laagers the Boers had religious services at daybreak and after sunset every day, whether they were near to the enemy or far away. At first the novelty of being awakened early in the morning by the voices of a large commando of burghers was not conducive to a religious feeling in the mind of the stranger, but a short stay in the laagers caused anger to turn to admiration. After sunset the burghers again gathered in groups around camp-fires, and made the countryside re-echo with the sound of their deep, bass voices united in Dutch hymns and psalms of praise and thanksgiving.

Whether they ate a big meal from a well-equipped table, or whether they leaped from their horses to make a hasty meal of biltong and bread, they reverently bowed their heads and asked a blessing before and after eating. Before they went into battle they gathered around their general and were led in prayer by the man who afterwards led them against the enemy. When the battle was concluded, and whether the field was won or lost, prayers were offered to the God of battles. In the reports which generals and commandants made to the war departments, victories and defeats were invariably ascribed to the will of God, and such phrases as "All the glory belongs to the Lord of Hosts who led us," and "God gave us the victory," and "Divine favour guided our footsteps," were frequent. When one is a stranger of the Boers and unacquainted with the simple faith which they place in Divine guidance, these religious manifestations may appear inopportune in warfare, but it is necessary to observe the Boer burgher in all his various actions and emotions to know that he is sincere in his religious beliefs and that he endeavours to be a Christian in deed as well as in word.

The Boer army, like Cromwell's troopers, could fight as well as pray, but in reality it was not a fighting organisation in the sense that warfare was agreeable to the burghers. The Boer proved that he could fight when there was a necessity for it, but to the great majority of them it was heartrending to slay their fellow human beings. The Boer's hand was better adapted to the stem of a pipe than to the stock of an army rifle, and he would rather have been engaged in the former peaceful pursuit had he not believed that it was a holy war in which he was engaged. That he was not eager for fighting was displayed in a hundred different ways. He loved his home more than the laagers at the front, and he took advantage of every opportunity to return to his home and family. He lusted not for battle, and he seldom engaged in one unless he firmly believed that success depended partly upon his individual presence. He did not go into battle because he had the lust of blood, for he abhorred the slaughter of men, and it was not an extraordinary spectacle to see a Boer weeping beside the corpse of a British soldier. On the field, after the Spion Kop battle, where Boer guns did their greatest execution, there were scores of bare-headed Boers who deplored the war, and amidst ejaculations of "Poor Tommy," and "This useless slaughter," brushed away the tears that rolled down over their brown cheeks and beards. Never a Boer was seen to exult over a victory. They might say "That is good" when they heard of a Spion Kop or a Magersfontein, but never a shout or any other of the ordinary methods of expressing joy. The foreigners in the army frequently were beside themselves with joy after victories, but the Boers looked stolidly on and never took any part in the demonstrations.

4. The Army Organisation

When the Boer goes on a lion-hunting expedition he must be thoroughly acquainted with the game country; he must be experienced in the use of the rifle, and he must know how to protect himself against the attacks of the enemy. When he is thus equipped and he abandons lion-hunting for the more strenuous life of war the Boer is a formidable enemy, for he has combined in him the qualities of a general as well as the powers of a private soldier. In lion-hunting the harm of having too many men in authority is not so fatal to the success of the expedition as it is in real warfare, where the enemy may have less generals but a larger force of men who will obey their commands. All the successes of the Boer army were the result of the fact that every burgher was a general, and to the same cause may be attributed almost every defeat. Whenever this army of generals combined and agreed to do a certain work it was successful, but it was unsuccessful whenever the generals disagreed. If the opportunity had given birth to a man who would have been accepted as general of the generals--a man was needed who could introduce discipline and training into the rudimentary military system of the country--the chances of the Boer success would have been far greater.

The leaders of the Boer army were elected by a vote of the people in the same manner in which they chose their presidents and civil officials. Age, ability, and military experience did not have any bearing on the subject except in so far as they influenced the mind of the individual voter. Family influences, party affiliations, and religion had a strong bearing on the result of the elections, and, as is frequently the case with civil authorities in other countries, the men with the best military minds and experience were not always chosen. It was as a result of this system that General Joubert was at the head of the army when a younger, more energetic, and more warlike man should have been Commandant-General. At the last election for Commandant-General, Joubert, a Progressive, also received the support of the Conservatives, so that two years later he might not be a candidate for the Presidency against Paul Kruger. In the same manner the commandants of the districts and the field-cornets of the wards were chosen, and in the majority of the cases no thought was taken of their military ability at the time of the election. The voters of a ward, the lowest political division in the country, elected their field-cornet more with a view of having him administer the laws in times of peace than with the idea of having him lead them into a battle, and in like manner the election of a commandant for a district, which generally consisted of five wards, was more of a victory for his popularity in peace than for his presumed bravery in war. The Boer system of electing military leaders by vote of the people may have had certain advantages, but it had the negative advantage of effacing all traces of authority between officers and men. The burgher who had assisted in electing his field-cornet felt that that official owed him a certain amount of gratitude for having voted for him, and obeyed his orders or disobeyed them whenever he chose to do so. The field-cornet represented authority over his men, but of real authority there was none. The commandants were presumed to have authority over the field-cornets and the generals over the commandants, but whether the authority was of any value could not be ascertained until after the will of those in lower rank was discovered. By this extraordinary process it happened that every burgher was a general and that no general was greater than a burgher.

The military officers of the Boers, with the exception of the Commandant-General, were the same men who ruled the country in times of peace. War suddenly transformed pruning-hooks into swords, and conservators of peace into leaders of armies. The head of the army was the Commandant-General, who was invested with full power to direct operations and lead men.

Directly under his authority were the Assistant Commandant-Generals, five of whom were appointed by the Volksraad a short time before the beginning of hostilities. Then in rank were those who were called Vecht-Generals, or fighting generals, in order to distinguish them from the Assistant-Generals. Then followed the Commandants, the leaders of the field-cornets of one district, whose rank was about that of colonels. The field-cornets, who were in command of the men of a ward, were under the authority of a commandant, and ranked on a par with majors. The burghers of every ward were subdivided into squads of about twenty-five men under the authority of a corporal, whose rank was equal to that of a lieutenant. There were no corps, brigades, regiments, and companies to call for hundreds of officers; it was merely a commando, whether it had ten men or ten thousand, and neither the subdivision nor the augmentation of a force affected the list of officers in any way. Nor would such a multiplication of officers weaken the fighting strength of a force, for every officer, from Commandant-General to corporal, carried and used a rifle in every battle.

ELECTING A FIELD-CORNET

When the officers had their men on the field, and desired to make a forward movement or an attack on the enemy, it was necessary to hold a Krijgsraad, or council of war, and this was conducted in such a novel way that the most unmilitary burgher's voice bore almost as much weight as that of the Commandant-General. Every officer, from corporal to Commandant-General, was a member of the Krijgsraad, and when a plan was favoured by the majority of those present at the council it became a law. The result of a Krijgsraad meeting did not necessarily imply that it was the plan favoured by the best military minds at the council, for it was possible and legal for the opinions of sixteen corporals to be adopted although fifteen generals and commandants opposed the plan with all their might. That there ever was such a result is problematical, but there were many Krijgsraads at which the opinion of the best and most experienced officers were cast aside by the votes of field-cornets and corporals. It undoubtedly was a representative way of adopting the will of the people, but it frequently was exceedingly costly. At the Krijgsraad in Natal which determined to abandon the positions along the Tugela, and retire north of Ladysmith the project was bitterly opposed by the generals who had done the bravest and best fighting in the colony, but the votes of the corporals, field-cornets, and commandants outnumbered theirs, and there was nothing for the generals to do but to retire and allow Ladysmith to be relieved. At Mafeking scores of Krijgsraad were held for the purpose of arriving at a determination to storm the town, but invariably the field-cornets and corporals out-voted the commandants and generals and refused to risk the lives of their men in such a hazardous attack. Even the oft-repeated commands of the Commandant-General to storm Mafeking were treated with contempt by the majority of the Krijgsraad who constituted the highest military authority in the country so far as they and their actions were concerned. When there happened to be a deadlock in the balloting at a Krijgsraad it was more than once the case that the vote of the Commandant-General counted for less than the voice of a burgher. In one of the minor Krijgsraads in Natal there was a tie in the voting, which was ended when an old burgher called his corporal aside and influenced him to change his vote. The Commandant-General himself had not been able to change the result of the voting, but the old burgher who had no connection with the council of war practically determined the result of the meeting.

The Krijgsraad was the supreme military authority in the country, and its resolutions were the law, all its infractions being punishable by fines. The minority of a Krijgsraad was obliged to assist in executing the plans of the majority, however impracticable or distasteful they might have been to those whose opinions did not prevail. There were innumerable instances where generals and commandants attended a Krijgsraad and afterward acted quite contrary to the resolution adopted by the council. In any other army such action would have been called disobedience of orders, with the corresponding punishment, but in the Boer army it amounted to little beyond personal animosity. According to Boer military law an officer offending in such a manner should have been arraigned before the Krijgsraad and tried by his fellow officers, but such occurrences were extremely rare.

One of the few instances where a man was arraigned before a Krijgsraad for dereliction of duty was after the enemy succeeded in damaging one of the "Long Tom's" around Ladysmith.

The artillery officer who was in charge of the gun when the dynamite was exploded in its muzzle was convicted of neglect of duty and was disgraced before the army. After the battle of Belmont Vecht-General Jacob Prinsloo, of the Free State, was court-martialled for cowardice and was reduced to the rank of burgher. It was Prinsloo's first battle, and he was thoroughly frightened. When some of his men came up to him and asked him for directions to repel the advancing British force Prinsloo trembled, rubbed his hands, and replied: "God only knows; I don't," and fled with all his men at his heels.

Two instances where commandants acted contrary to the decisions of Krijgsraad were the costly disobedience of General Erasmus, at Dundee, and the still more costly mistake of Commandant Buis at Hlangwe. When the Boers invaded Natal and determined to attack the British forces then stationed at the town of Dundee, it was decided at a Krijgsraad that General Lucas Meyer should attack from the east and south, and General Erasmus from the north. General Meyer occupied Talana Hill, east of Dundee, and a kopje south of the town, and attacked General Penn-Symons's forces at daybreak. General Erasmus and the Pretoria commando, with field pieces and a "Long Tom," occupied Impati Mountain on the north, but when the time arrived for him to assist in the attack on the enemy several hundred yards below him he would not allow one shot to be fired. As a result of the miscarriage of plans General Meyer was compelled to retire from Talana Hill in the afternoon, while the British force was enabled to escape southward into Ladysmith. If General Erasmus had followed the decision of the Krijgsraad, and had assisted in the attack, there is hardly any doubt that the entire force of the enemy would have been captured. Even more disastrous was the disobedience of Commandant Buis, of the Heidelberg commando, who was ordered to occupy a certain point on the Boschrand, called Hlangwe, about February 19th. The British had tried for several weeks to drive the Boers from the Boschrand, but all their attempts proved fruitless. A certain commando had been holding Hlangwe for a long time, and Commandant Buis was ordered to take his commando and relieve the others by night. Instead of going to Hlangwe immediately that night he bivouacked in a small nek near by, intending to occupy the position early the following morning. During the night the British discovered that the point was unoccupied and placed a strong force there. In this manner the British wedge was forced into the Boschrand, and shortly afterwards the Boers were obliged to retreat across the Tugela and secure positions on the north bank of the stream. Of less serious consequence was General De la Rey's refusal to carry out a decision he himself had assisted in framing. It was at Brandfort, in the Free State, several weeks after Bloemfontein was occupied, and all the Boer generals in the vicinity met in Krijgsraad and voted to make a concerted attack upon the British force at Tafelkop, midway between Bloemfontein and Brandfort. Generals Smuts and Botha made a long night trek to the positions from which they were to attack the enemy at daybreak. It had been arranged that

General De la Rey's commando should open the attack from another point, and that no operations should begin until after he had given a certain signal. The signal was never given, and, after waiting for it several hours, the other generals returned to Brandfort only to find that General De la Rey had not even moved from his laager.

When the lower ranks of officers--the field-cornets and corporals--disobeyed the mandates of the Krijgsraads, displayed cowardice or misbehaved in any other manner, the burghers under their command were able to impeach them and elect other officers to fill the vacancies. The corporals were elected by the burghers after war was begun, and they held their posts only so long as their behaviour met with the favour of those who placed them in authority. During the first three months of the war innumerable changes of that nature were made, and not infrequently was it the case that a corporal was unceremoniously dismissed because he had offended one of his men who happened to wield much influence over his fellows in the commando. Personal popularity had much to do with the tenure of office, but personal bravery was not allowed to go unrewarded, and it happened several times in the laagers along the Tugela that a corporal resigned his rank so that one of his friends who had distinguished himself in a battle might have his work recognised and appreciated.

However independent and irresponsible the Boer officer may have been, he was a man in irons compared with the Boer burgher. The burgher was bound by no laws except such as he made for himself. There was a State law which compelled him to join a commando and to accompany it to the front, or in default of that law to pay a small fine. As soon as he was "on commando," as he called it, he became his own master and could laugh at Mr. Atkins across the way who was obliged to be constantly attending to various camp duties when not actively engaged. No general, no act of Volksraad could compel him to do any duty if he felt uninclined to perform it, and there was no power on earth which could compel him to move out of his tent if he did not desire to go. In the majority of countries a man may volunteer to join the army but when once he is a soldier he is compelled to fight, but in the Boer country the man was compelled to join the army, but he was not obliged to fight unless he volunteered to do so. There were hundreds of men in the Natal laagers who never engaged in one battle and never fired a shot in the first six months of the war. Again, there were hundreds of men who took part in almost every one of the battles, whether their commando was engaged or not, but they joined the fighting voluntarily and not because they were compelled to do so.

When a Krijgsraad determined to make or resist an attack it was decided by the officers at the meeting how many men were needed for the work. Immediately after the meeting the officers returned to their commandos, and, after explaining to their burghers the nature and object of the expedition, asked for volunteers. The officer could not call upon certain men and order them to take part in the purposed proceedings he could only ask them to volunteer their services. It happened at times that an entire commando of several hundred men volunteered to do the work asked of them, but just as often it happened that only from one-tenth to one-twentieth of the burghers expressed their willingness to accompany the expedition. Several days after the Spion Kop battle General Botha called for four hundred volunteers to assist in resisting an attack that it was feared would be made. There were almost ten thousand men in the environs of Ladysmith at that time, but it was with the utmost difficulty that the four hundred men could be gathered. Two hundred men came from one commando, one hundred and fifty-three from another, twenty-eight from a third, fifteen from another, and five from another made a total of four hundred and one men--one more than was called for.

When Commandant-General Joubert, at his Hoofd--or head-laager at Modderspruit, received an urgent request for reinforcements he was not able to order one of the commandos that was in laager near him to go to the assistance of the fighting burghers; he could only make a request of the different commandants and field-cornets to ask their men to volunteer for the service. If the men refused to go, then naturally the reinforcements could not be sent, and those who were in dire need of assistance had the alternative of continuing the struggle alone or of yielding a position to the enemy. The relief of Ladysmith was due to the fact that Generals Botha, Erasmus, and Meyer could not receive reinforcements from Commandant-General Joubert, who was north of Ladysmith with almost ten thousand men. Botha, Meyer, and Erasmus had been fighting for almost a week without a day's intermission, and their two thousand men were utterly exhausted when Joubert was asked to send reinforcements, or even men enough to relieve those from fighting for a day or two, but a Krijgsraad had decided that the entire army should retreat to the Biggarsberg, and Joubert could not, or at least would not, send any burghers to the Tugela, with the result that Botha was compelled to retreat and abandon positions which could have been held indefinitely if there had been military discipline in the commandos. It was not always the case that commandants and generals were obliged to go begging for volunteers, and there were innumerable times when every man of a commando did the work assigned to him without a murmur.

During the Natal campaign the force was so large, and the work seemed so comparatively easy that the majority of the burghers never went to the firing line, but when British successes in the Free State placed the Boers on the defensive it was not so easy to remain behind in the laagers and allow others more willing to engage in the fighting. General Cronje was able to induce a much larger percentage of his men to fight than Commandant-General Joubert, but the reasons for this were that he was much firmer with his men and that he moved from one place to another more frequently than Joubert. Towards the end of General Cronje's campaign all his men were willing to enter a battle, but that was because they realised that they must fight, and in that there was much that was lacking in the Natal army. When a Boer realised that he must fight or lose his life or a battle, he would fight as few other men were able to fight, but when he imagined that his presence at the firing line was not imperative he chose to remain in laager.

KRIJGSRAAD, NEAR THABA N'CHU

There were hundreds of burghers who took part in almost every battle in Natal, and these were the individuals who understood the frame of mind of some of their countrymen, and determined that they must take upon themselves the responsibilities of fighting and winning battles. Among those who were most forward in fighting were the Johannesburg police, the much-despised "Zarps" of peaceful times; the Pretoria commando, and the younger men of other commandos. There were many old Boers who left their laagers whenever they heard the report of a gun, but the ages of the great majority of those who were killed or injured were between seventeen and thirty years. After the British captured Bloemfontein, and the memorable Krijgsraad at Kroonstad determined that guerilla warfare should be followed thereafter, it was not an easy matter for a burgher to remain behind in the laagers, for the majority of the ox-wagons and other camp paraphernalia was sent home and laager life was not so attractive as before. Commandos remained at one place only a short time, and there was almost a daily opportunity for a brush with the enemy. The war had been going on for six months, but many of the men had their first taste of actual war as late as that, and, after the first battle had been safely passed through, the following ones were thought of little consequence. When General Christian De Wet began his campaign in the eastern part of the Free State there were hardly enough men left in the laagers to guard them properly when battles were in progress, and in the battles at Sannaspost, Moester's Hoek, and Wepener probably ninety-nine per cent. of his men took part in every battle. In Natal the real fighting spirit was lacking from the majority of the men, or Commandant-General Joubert might never have been wiped aside from the path to Durban; but months afterward, when the burgher learned that his services were actually needed, and that, if he did not fight, he was liable to be captured and sent to St. Helena, he polished his Mauser and fought as hard and well as he was able.

The same carelessness or indifference which manifested itself throughout the early part of the Natal campaign with regard to the necessity of assisting in the fighting was evident in that all-important part of an army's work, the guarding of the laagers. The Boers did not have sentries or outposts as they are understood in trained armies, but they had what was called a "Brandwacht," or fire-guard, which consisted of a hundred men or more who were supposed to take positions at a certain distance from the laagers, and remain there until daybreak. These men were volunteers secured by the corporal, who was responsible to his field-cornet for a certain number of men every night. It was never made compulsory upon any one to go on Brandwacht, but the duty was not considered irksome, and there were always as many volunteers as were required for the work.

The men on Brandwacht carried with them blankets, pipes, and kettles, and, after reaching the point which they were to occupy during the night, they tethered their horse to one of their feet and made themselves comfortable with pipe and coffee. When the enemy was known to be near by the Brandwacht kept awake, as a matter of personal safety, but when there seemed to be no danger of attack he fastened his blankets around his body and, using his saddle for a pillow, slept until the sun rose. There was a mild punishment for those who slept while on this duty, and occasionally the burgher found in the morning that some one had extracted the bolt of his rifle during the night. When the corporal produced the bolt as evidence against him in the morning and sentenced him to carry a stone or a box of biscuits on his head the burgher might decline to be punished, and no one could say aught against his determination.

The Boer scouts, or spies as they called them, received their finest tribute from Sir George White, the British Commander at Ladysmith. In a speech which he delivered at Cape Town, Sir George said--

"All through this campaign, from the first day the Boers crossed the frontier to the relief of Ladysmith, I and others who have been in command near me, have been hampered by their excellent system of intelligence, for which I give them all credit. I wish to goodness that they had neglected it, for I could not move a gun, even if I did not give the order till midnight, but they knew it by daylight next morning. And they had their agents, who gave them their intelligence through thick and thin. I locked up everybody who I thought could go and tell, but somehow or other the intelligence went on."

The Boer was an effective scout because he was familiar with the country, and because his eyes were far better than those of any of the men against whom he was pitted. The South African atmosphere is extraordinarily clear, and every person has a long range of vision, but the Boer, who was accustomed to the climatic conditions, could distinguish between Boer and Briton where the stranger could barely see a moving object. Field-glasses were almost valueless to Boer scouts, and few of them were carried by any one except the generals and commandants, who secured them from the War Department before the beginning of the war. There was no distinct branch of the army whose exclusive duty it was to scout, and there was even greater lack of organisation in the matter of securing information concerning the movements of the enemy than in the other departments of the army's work. When a general or commandant felt that it was necessary to secure accurate information concerning the enemy's strength and whereabouts he asked for volunteers to do the work. Frequently, during the Natal campaign, no scouting was done for days, and the generals were absolutely ignorant of everything in connection with the enemy. Later in the campaign several scouting corps composed of foreign volunteers were organised, and thereafter the Boers depended wholly upon the information they secured. There was no regulation which forbade burghers from leaving the laagers at any time, or from proceeding in any direction, and much of the information that reached the generals was obtained from these rovers over the veld. It was extremely difficult for a man who did not have the appearance of a burgher to ride over the veld for more than a mile without being hailed by a Boer who seemed to have risen out of the earth unnoticed. "Where are you going?" or "Where are you coming from?" were his invariable salutations, and if the stranger was unable to give a satisfactory reply or show proper passports he was commanded, "Hands up." The burghers were constantly on the alert when they were on the veld, whether they were merely wandering about, leaving for home, or returning to the laager, and as soon as they secured any information which they believed was valuable they dashed away to the nearest telegraph or heliograph station, and reported it to their general or commandant. In addition to this valuable attribute the Boers had the advantage of being among white and black friends who could assist them in a hundred different ways in securing information concerning the enemy, and all these circumstances combined to warrant General White's estimate of the Boers' intelligence department, which, notwithstanding its efficiency, was more or less chimerical.

In no department or branch of the army was there any military discipline or system, except in the two small bodies of men known as the State Artillery of the Transvaal and the State Artillery of the Free State. These organisations were in existence many years before the war was begun, and had regular drills and practice which were maintained when they were at the front. The Johannesburg Police also had a form of discipline which, however, was not strict enough to prevent the men from becoming mutinous when they imagined that they had fought the whole war themselves, and wanted to have a vacation in order that they might visit their homes. The only vestige of real military discipline that was to be found in the entire Boer army was that which was maintained by Field-Cornet A.L. Thring, of the Kroonstad commando, who had a roll-call and inspection of rifles every morning. This extraordinary procedure was not relished by the burghers, who made an indignant protest to General Christian De Wet. The general upheld the field-cornet's action, and told the men that if all the officers had instituted similar methods more success might have attended the army's operations.

With the exception of the instances cited, every man was a disciplinary law unto himself, and when he transgressed that law no one would punish him but his conscience. There were laws on the subject of obedience in the army, and each had penalties attached to it, but it was extremely rare that a burgher was punished. When he endured discipline he did it because he cared to do so, and not because he feared those who had authority over him. He was deeply religious, and he felt that in being obedient he was finding favour in the eyes of the Providence that favoured his cause. It was as much his religion as his ability to aim unerringly that made the Boer a good soldier. If the Boer army had been composed of an irreligious, undisciplined body of men, instead of the psalm-singing farmers, it would have been conquered by itself. The religion of the Boers was their discipline.

5. The Boer Military System

The disparity between the British and Boer armies seemed to be so great at the time the war was begun that the patriotic Englishman could hardly be blamed for asserting that the struggle would be of only a month's duration. On the one side was an army every branch of which was highly developed and specialised and kept in constant practice by many wars waged under widely different conditions. Back of it was a great nation, with millions of men and unlimited resources to draw upon. At the head of the army were men who had the theory and practice of warfare as few leaders of other armies had had the opportunities of securing them. Opposed to this army was practically an aggregation of farmers, hastily summoned together and utterly without discipline or training. They were unable to replace with another a single fallen burgher and prevented from adding by importation to their stock of ammunition a single rifle or a single pound of powder. At the head were farmers who, perhaps, did not know that there existed a theory of warfare and much less knew how recent wars were fought and won. The means by which thirty thousand farmers of no military training were enabled to withstand the opposition of several hundred thousand well-trained soldiers for the greater part of a year must be attributed to the military system which gave such a marvellous advantage. Such success as attended the Boer army was undoubtedly the success of its system of warfare against that of the British.

BOER COMMANDANTS READING MESSAGE FROM BRITISH
OFFICERS AFTER THE BATTLE OF DUNDEE

The Boers themselves were not aware that they had a military system; at least, none of the generals or men acknowledged the existence of such, and it was not an easy matter to find evidences that battles were fought and movements made according to certain established rules which suggested a system. The Boers undoubtedly had a military plan of their own which was naturally developed in their many wars with natives and with the British troops. It might not have been a system, according to the correct definition of the term--it might have been called an instinct for fighting, or a common-sense way of attempting to defeat an enemy--but it was a matter which existed in the mind of every single citizen of the two Republics. It was not to be learned from books or teachers, nor could it be taught to those who were not born in the country. Whatever that system was, it was extremely rudimentary, and was never developed to any extent by the discipline and training which any system necessarily requires in order to make it effective. There was a natural system or manner used by the Boers when hunting for lion or buck, and it was identically the same which they applied against the British army. Every Boer was expert in the use of his rifle; he had an excellent eye for country and cover; he was able to tell at a glance whether a hill or an undulation in the ground was suitable for fighting purposes, whether it could be defended and whether it offered facilities for attack or retreat. Just as every Boer was a general, so it was that every burgher had in his mind a certain military plan fashioned after the needs and opportunities of the country, and this was their system--a sort of national as well as natural military system.

In the British army, as well as in the other modern armies, the soldier is supposed to understand nothing, know nothing, and do nothing but give obedience to the commands of his officers. The trained soldier learns little, and is supposed to learn little, of anything except the evolutions he is taught on the drill-grounds. It is presumed that he is stupid, and the idea appears to be to prevent him from being otherwise in order that he may the better fulfil his part in the great machine to which a trained army has been likened. The soldier is regarded as an animal of low mental grade, whose functions are merely to obey the orders of the man who has been chosen by beings of superior intelligence to lead him. When the man who was chosen in times of peace to lead the men in times of war meets the enemy and fails to make a display of the military knowledge which it was presumed he possessed, then the soldiers who look to him for leadership are generally useless, and oftentimes worse than useless, inasmuch as their panic is likely to become infectious among neighbouring bodies of soldiers who are equipped with better leaders. In trained armies the value of a soldier is a mere reflection of the value of the officer who commands him, and the value of the army is relatively as great as the ability of its generals. In the Boer army the generals and commandants were of much less importance, for the reason that the Boer burgher acted almost always on his own initiative. The generals were of more service before the beginning of a battle than while it was in progress. When a burgher became aware of the presence of the enemy his natural instincts, his innate military system, told him the best manner in which to attack his adversary as well as his general could have informed him. The generals and other officers were of prime importance in leading the burghers to the point where the enemy was likely to be found, but when that point was reached their period of usefulness ended, for the burghers knew how to wage the battle as well as they did. Generally speaking, the most striking difference between the Boer army and a trained army was the difference in the distribution of intelligence.

All the intelligence of a trained army is centred in the officers; in the Boer army there was much practical military sense and alertness of mind distributed throughout the entire force.

Mr. Disraeli once said: "Doubtless to think with vigour, with clearness, and with depth in the recess of a cabinet is a fine intellectual demonstration; but to think with equal vigour, clearness, and depth among bullets, appears the loftiest exercise and the most complete triumph of the human faculties." Without attempting to insinuate that every Boer burgher was a man of the high mental attainments referred to by the eminent British statesman, it must be acknowledged that the fighting Boer was a man of more than ordinary calibre.

In battle the Boer burgher was practically his own general. He had an eye which quickly grasped a situation, and he never waited for an order from an officer to take advantage of it. When he saw that he could with safety approach the enemy more closely he did so on his own responsibility, and when it became evident to him that it would be advantageous to occupy a different position in order that he might stem the advance of the enemy he acted entirely on his own initiative. He remained in one position just as long as he considered it safe to do so, and if conditions warranted he went forward, and if they were adverse he retreated, whether there was an order from an officer or not. When he saw that the burghers in another part of the field were hard pressed by the enemy he deserted his own position and went to their assistance, and when his own position became untenable, in his own opinion, he simply vacated it and went to another spot where bullets and shells were less thick. If he saw a number of the enemy who were detached from the main body of their own force, and he believed that they could be taken prisoner, he enlisted a number of the burghers who were near him, and made an effort to capture them, whether there was an officer close at hand or a mile distant.

No one was surfeited with orders; in fact, the lack of them was more noticeable, and it was well that it was so, for the Boer burgher disliked to be ordered, and he always did things with better grace when he acted spontaneously. An illustration of this fact was an incident at the fight of Modderspruit where two young Boers saved an entire commando from falling into the hands of the enemy. Lieutenant Oelfse, of the State Artillery, and Reginald Sheppard, of the Pretoria commando, observed a strong force of the British advancing towards a kopje where the Krugersdorp commando was concealed. The two men saw that the Krugersdorpers would be cut off in a short time if they were not informed of the British advance, so they determined to plunge across the open veld, six hundred yards from the enemy's guns, and tell them of their danger. No officer could have compelled the men to undertake such a hazardous journey across a bullet-swept plain, but Oelfse and Sheppard acted on their own responsibility, succeeded in reaching the Krugersdorp commando without being hit, and gave to the commandant the information which undoubtedly saved him and his men from being captured. Incidents of like nature occurred in almost every battle of the campaign, and occasionally the service rendered so voluntarily by the burghers was of momentous consequences, even if the act itself seemed trivial at the time.

A second feature of the Boer army, and equally as important as the freedom of action of its individuals, was its mobility. Every burgher was mounted on a fleet horse or pony, and consequently his movements on the battlefield, whether in an advance or in a retreat, were many times more rapid that those of his enemy--an advantage which was of inestimable value both during an engagement and in the intervals between battles when it was necessary to secure new positions. During the progress of a battle the Boers were able to desert a certain point for a time, mount their horses and ride to another position, and throw their full strength against the latter, yet remaining in such close touch with the former that it was possible to return and defend it in an exceedingly short space of time. With the aid of their horses they could make such a sudden rush from one position to another that the infantry of the enemy could be surrounded and cut off from all communications with the body of its army almost before it was known that any Boers were in the vicinity, and it was due to that fact that the Boers were able to make so many large numbers of captives.

The fighting along the Tugela furnished many magnificent examples of the Boers' extreme mobility. There it was a constant jump from one position to another--one attack here yesterday, another there to-day. It was an incessant movement made necessary by the display of energy by the British, whose thrice-larger forces kept the Boers in a state of continued ferment. On one side of the river, stretched out from the south of Spion Kop, in the west, to almost Helpmakaar, in the east, were thirty thousand British troops watching for a weak point where they might cross, and attacking whenever there seemed to be the slightest opportunity of breaking through; on the other side were between two and three thousand mounted Boers, jumping from one point to another in the long line of territory to be guarded, and repelling the attacks whenever they were made. The country was in their favour, it is true, but it was not so favourable that a handful of men could defend it against thousands, and it was partly due to the great ease and rapidity with which the Boers could move from one place to another, that Ladysmith remained besieged so long. The mobility of the Boers was again well demonstrated by the retreat of the burghers from the environs of Ladysmith. After the Krijgsraad decided to withdraw the forces into the Biggarsberg, it required only a few hours for all the many commandos to leave the positions they had held so long; to load their impedimenta and to be well on the way to the northward. The departure was so rapid that it surprised even those who were in Ladysmith. One day the Boers were shelling the town as usual and all the commandos were observed in the same positions which they had occupied for several months; the following day not a single Boer was to be seen anywhere. They had quietly mounted their horses by night and before the sun rose in the morning they were trekking north beyond Modderspruit and Elandslaagte, on the way to Glencoe. General Cronje's flight from Magersfontein was also accomplished with great haste and in good order, but what probably was the finest example of the Boers' mobility was the magnificent retreat along the Basuto border of Generals Grobler, Olivier, and Lemmer, with their six thousand men, when the enemy was known to be in great strength within several days' march of them. After the capture of Cronje at Paardeberg the three generals, who had been conducting the campaign in the eastern provinces of Cape Colony, were in a most dangerous position, having the enemy in the rear, the left and left front, the neutral Basuto land on the right front, and only a small strip of territory along the western border of the Basuto country apparently free of the enemy. The British were in Bloemfontein and in the surrounding country, and it seemed almost impossible that the six thousand men could ever extricate themselves from such a position to join the Boer forces in the north. It would have been a comparatively easy matter for six thousand mounted men to make the journey if they had not been loaded down with impedimenta, but the three generals were obliged to carry with them all their huge transport wagons and heavy camping paraphernalia. The trek northward was begun near Colesburg on March 12th, and when all the different commandos had joined the main column the six thousand horsemen, the seven hundred and fifty transport-wagons, the two thousand natives, and twelve thousand cattle formed a line extending more than twenty-four miles. The scouts, who were despatched westward from the column to ascertain the whereabouts of the enemy, reported large forces of British cavalry sixty and seventy miles distant, but for some inexplicable reason the British made no attempt to cut off the retreat of the three generals, and on March 28th they reached Kroonstad, having traversed almost four hundred miles of territory in the comparatively short time of sixteen days. Sherman's march to the sea was made under extraordinary conditions, but the retreat of the three generals was fraught with dangers and difficulties much greater. Sherman passed through a fertile country, and had an enemy which was disheartened. The three generals had an enemy flushed with its first victories, while the country through which they passed was mountainous and muddy. If the column had been captured so soon after the Paardeberg disaster, the relief of Kimberley and the relief of Ladysmith, it might have been so disheartening to the remaining Boer commandos that the war might have been ended at that time. It was a magnificent retreat and well worthy to be placed in the Boer's scroll of honour with Cronje's noble stand at Paardeberg, with Spion Kop and Magersfontein.

GENERAL GROBLER

The Boer army was capable of moving rapidly under almost any conditions. The British army demonstrated upon many occasions that it could not move more than two or three miles an hour when the column was hampered with transport wagons and camping paraphernalia, and frequently it was impossible to proceed at that pace for many consecutive hours. A Boer commando easily travelled six miles an hour and not infrequently, when there was a necessity for rapid motion, seven and even eight miles an hour were traversed. When General Lucas Meyer moved his commandos along the border at the outset of the war and learned that General Penn-Symons was located at Dundee he made a night march of almost forty miles in six hours and occupied Talana Hill, a mile distant from the enemy, who was ignorant of the Boers' proximity until the camp was shelled at daybreak. When General De Wet learned that Colonel Broadwood was moving westward from Thaba N'Chu on March 30th, he was in laager several miles east of Brandfort, but it required only several minutes for all the burghers to be on their horses and ready to proceed toward the enemy. The journey of twenty-five miles to Sannaspost, or the Bloemfontein waterworks, was made in the short time of five hours, while Colonel Broadwood's forces consumed seven hours in making the ten miles' journey from Thaba N'Chu to the same place. The

British column was unable to move more rapidly on account of its large convoy of wagons, but even then the rate of progress was not as great as that made by the trekking party of the three generals who were similarly hampered. It was rarely the case that the Boers attempted to trek for any considerable distance with their heavy wagons when they were aware of the presence of the enemy in the vicinity. Ox-wagons were always left behind, while only a small number of mule-wagons, bearing provisions and ammunition, were taken, and on that account they were able to move with greater rapidity than their opponents. Frequently they entered dangerous territory with only a few days' provisions and risked a famine of food and ammunition rather than load themselves down with many lumbering wagons which were likely to retard their progress. After fighting the battle at Moester's Hoek, General De Wet had hardly three days' food and very little ammunition with him, yet rather than delay his march and send for more wagons, he proceeded to Wepener where, after several days' fighting, both his food and ammunition became exhausted and he was obliged to lie idle around the enemy and await the arrival of the supplies which he might have carried with him at the outset of the trek if he had cared to risk such an impediment to his rapid movements.

One of the primary reasons why the Boer could move more rapidly than the British was the difference in the weight carried by their horses. The Boer paid no attention to art when he went to war, and consequently he carried nothing that was not absolutely essential. His saddle was less than half the weight of a British saddle, and that was almost all the equipment he carried when on a trek. The Boer rider and equipment, including saddle, rifle, blankets, and a food-supply, rarely weighed more than two hundred and fifty pounds, which was not a heavy load for a horse to carry. A British cavalryman and his equipment of heavy saddle, sabre, carbine, and saddle-bags, rarely weighed less than four hundred pounds--a burden which soon tired a horse. Again, almost every Boer had two horses, so that when one had been ridden for an hour or more he was relieved and led, while the other was used. In this manner the Boers were able to travel from twelve to fourteen hours in a day when it was absolutely necessary to reach a certain point at a given time. Six miles an hour was the rate of progress ascribed to horses in normal condition, and when a forced march was attempted they could travel sixty and seventy miles in a day, and be in good condition the following morning to undertake another journey of equal length. Small commandos often covered sixty and seventy miles in a day, especially during the fighting along the Tugela, while after the battles of Poplar Grove and Abraham's Kraal, and the capture of Bloemfontein, it seemed as if the entire army in the Free State were moving northward at a rate of speed far exceeding that of an express train.

The mobility of the Boer army was then on a par with that of the British army after the battle of Dundee, and it was difficult to determine which of the two deserved the palm for the best display of accelerated motion.

A feature of the Boer system of warfare which was most striking was the manner in which each individual protected himself, as far as possible, from danger. In lion-hunting it is an axiom that the hunter must not pursue a wounded lion into tall grass or underbrush lest the pursuer may be attacked. In the Boer army it was a natural instinct, common to all the burghers, which led them to seek their own safety whenever danger seemed to be near. Men who follow the most peaceful pursuits of life value their lives highly. They do not assume great risks even if great ends are to be attained. The majority of the Boers were farmers who saw no glory in attempting to gain a great success, the attainment of which made it necessary that they should risk their lives. It seemed as if each man realised that his death meant a great loss to the Boer army, already small, and that he did not mean to diminish its size if he could possibly prevent it. The Boer was quick in noting when the proper time arrived for retreat, and he was not slothful in acting upon his observations. Retreating at the proper time was one of the Boers' characteristics, but it could not be called an advantage, for frequently many of the Boers misjudged the proper time for retreating and left the field when a battle was almost won. At Poplar Grove the Boers might have won the day if the majority of the burghers had remained and fought an hour or two longer instead of retreating precipitately when the individuals determined that safety was to be found only in flight. At Elandslaagte the foreigners under General Kock did not gauge the proper moment for retreat, but continued with the fighting and were almost annihilated by the Lancers because of their lack of discretion in that respect. The burghers of the Free State, in particular, had the instinct of retreating abnormally developed, and whenever a battle was in progress large numbers of burghers could be observed going in an opposite direction as rapidly as their ponies could carry them over the veld. The lack of discipline in the commandos made such practices possible; in fact there was no rule or law by which a burgher could be prevented from retreating or deserting whenever he felt that he did not care to participate in a battle. After the British occupation of Bloemfontein there was a small skirmish about eight miles north of that city at a place called Tafelkop which sent the Free Staters running in all directions. The veld seemed to be filled with deserters, and at every farmhouse there were from two to six able-bodied men who had retreated when they believed themselves to be in grave danger.

Foolish men attribute all the moral courage in the world to the soldiers of their own country, but nature made a wise distribution of that gift, and not all the

Boers were cowards. Boer generals with only a few hundred men time and again attacked thousands of British soldiers, and frequently vanquished them. General Botha's twenty-five hundred men held out for a week against General Buller's thirty or forty thousand men, and General Cronje with his four thousand burghers succumbed to nothing less than forty thousand men and a hundred and fifty heavy guns under Field-Marshal Lord Roberts. Those two examples of Boer bravery would suffice to prove that the South African farmers had moral courage of no mean order if there were not a thousand and one other splendid records of bravery. The burghers did not always lie behind their shelter until the enemy had come within several hundred yards and then bowl them over with deadly accuracy. At the Platrand fight near Ladysmith, on January 6th, the Boers charged and captured British positions, drove the defenders out, and did it so successfully that only a few Boers were killed. The Spion Kop fight, a second Majuba Hill, was won after one of the finest displays of moral courage in the war. It requires bravery of the highest type for a small body of men to climb a steep hill in the face of the enemy which is three times greater numerically and armed with larger and more guns, yet that was the case with the Boers at Spion Kop. There were but few battles in the entire campaign that the Boer forces were not vastly outnumbered by the enemy, who usually had from twice to twenty times their number of cannon, yet the burghers were well aware of the fact and did not allow it to interfere with their plans nor did they display great temerity in battling with such a foe. When Lord Roberts and his three thousand cavalry entered Jacobsdal there were less than one hundred armed Boers in the town, but they made a determined stand against the enemy, and in a street-fight a large percentage of the burghers fell, and their blood mingled with that of those they had slain. Large bodies of Boers rarely attacked, and never resisted the enemy on level stretches of veld, not because they lacked courage to do so, but because they saw the futility of such action. After the British drove the Boers out of the kopjes east and north-east of Bloemfontein the burghers had no broken country suited to their particular style of warfare, and they retreated to the Vaal without much effort to stop the advance of the enemy. The Boer generals knew that the British were equipped with innumerable cannon, which could sweep the level veld for several miles before them and make the ground untenable for the riflemen--the mainstay of the Boer army.

When they were on hills the Boers were able to entrench themselves so thoroughly that the fire of several hundred heavy guns made hardly any impression on them, but as soon as they attempted to apply those tactics on level ground the results were most disastrous. At Colenso and Magersfontein the burghers remained in their trenches on the hills while thousands of shrapnel and other shells exploded above and around them, but very few men were injured, and when the British infantry advanced under cover of the shell fire the Boers merely remained in the trenches until the enemy had approached to within several hundred yards and then assailed them with rifle fire. Trenches always afforded perfect safety from shell fire, and on that account the Boers were able to cope so long and well with the British in the fighting along the Tugela and around Kimberley. The Boers generally remained quietly in their trenches and made no reply to the British cannon fire, however hot it was. The British generals several times mistook this silence as an indication that the Boers had evacuated the trenches, and sent forward bodies of infantry to occupy the positions. When the infantry reached the Boer zone of fire they usually met with a terrific Mauser fire that could not be stemmed, however gallant the attacks might have been. Hundreds of British soldiers lost their lives while going forward under shell fire to occupy a position which, it was presumed by the generals, was unoccupied by the Boers.

SPION KOP, WHERE BOERS CHARGED UP THE HILLSIDE

There were innumerable instances, also, of extraordinarily brave acts by individual burghers, but it was extremely difficult to hear of them owing to the Boers' disinclination to discuss a battle in its details. No Boer ever referred to his exploits or those of his friends of his own volition, and then only in the most indefinite manner. He related the story of a battle in much the same manner he told of the tilling of his fields or the herding of his cattle, and when there was any part of it pertaining to his own actions he passed it over without comment. It seemed as if every one was fighting, not for his own glorification, but for the success of his country's army, and consequently there was little hero-worship. Individual acts of bravery entitled the fortunate person to have his name mentioned in the *Staats-Courant*, the Government gazette, but hardly any attention was paid to the search for heroes, and only the names of a few men were even chronicled in the columns of that periodical. One of the bravest men in the Natal campaign was a young Pretoria burgher named Van Gas, who, in his youth, had an accident which made it necessary that his right arm should be amputated at the elbow. Later in life he was injured in one of the native wars and the upper arm was amputated, so that when he joined a commando he had only the left arm. It was an extraordinary spectacle to observe young Van Gaz holding his carbine between his knees while loading it with cartridges, and quite as strange to see the energy with which he discharged his rifle with one hand. He was in the van of the storming party at Spion Kop, where a bullet passed completely through his chest. He continued, however, to work his rifle between his knees and to shoot with his left arm, and was one of the first men to reach the summit of the hill, where he snatched the rifles from the hands of two British soldiers. After the battle was won he was carried to a hospital by several other burghers, but a month afterwards he was again at the front at the Tugela, going into exposed positions and shouting, "Come on, fellows, here is a good chance!" His companions desired to elect him as their field-cornet, but he refused the honour.

Evert Le Roux and Herculaas Nel, of the Swaziland Police, and two of the best scouts in the Boer army, were constantly engaged in recklessly daring enterprises, none of which, however, was quite equal to their actions on April 21st, when the vicinity of Ladysmith had been in British hands for almost two months. The two men went out on patrol and by night crept up a kopje behind which about three hundred British cavalrymen were bivouacking. The men were twenty miles distant from their laagers at Dundee and only a short distance from Ladysmith, but they lay down and slept on the other side of the kopje, less than a hundred yards from the cavalrymen. In the morning the British cavalry was divided into three squads, and all started for Ladysmith. Le Roux and Nel swept down toward the last squad, and called, "Hands up," to one of the men in the van. The cavalryman promptly held up his hands and a minute afterward surrendered his gun and himself, while the remainder of the squad fled precipitately. The two scouts, with their prisoner, quickly made a *détour* of another kopje, and appeared in front of the first squad, of whom they made a similar demand. One of the cavalrymen, who was in advance of the others, surrendered without attempting to make any resistance, while the others turned quickly to the right and rode headlong into a deep sloot. Le Roux shot the horse of one of the men before he reached the sloot, loaded the unhorsed man on one of the other prisoner's horses, and then pursued the fleeing cavalrymen almost to the city-limits of Ladysmith.

Major Albrecht, the head of the Free State-Artillery, was one of the bravest men in General Cronje's commando, and his display of courage at the battle of Magersfontein was not less extraordinary than that which he made later in the river bed at Paardeberg. At Magersfontein Albrecht and two of his artillerymen operated the cannon which were located behind schanzes twenty feet apart. The British had more than thirty cannon, which they turned upon the Boer cannon whenever one of them was discharged. After a short time the fire became so hot that Albrecht sent his assistants to places of safety, and operated the guns alone. For eight hours the intrepid Free State artilleryman jumped from one cannon to another, returning the fire whenever there was a lull in the enemy's attack and seeking safety behind the schanze when shells were falling too rapidly. It was an uneven contest, but the bravery of the one man inspired the others, and the end of the day saw the Boers nearer victory than they were in the morning. At Tafelkop, on March 30th, three burghers were caught napping by three British soldiers, who suddenly appeared before them and shouted, "Hands up!" While the soldiers were advancing toward them the three burghers succeeded in getting their rifles at their captors' heads, and turned the tables by making prisoners of them. There were many such instances of bravery, but one that is almost incredible occurred at the place called Railway Hill, near the Tugela, on February 24th. On that day the Boers did not appear to know anything concerning the position of the enemy, and James Marks, a Rustenburg farmer, determined to go out of the laager and reconnoitre on his own responsibility. Marks was more than sixty-two years old, and was somewhat decrepit, a circumstance which did not prevent him from taking part in almost every one of the Natal battles, however. The old farmer had been absent from his laager less than an hour when he saw a small body of British soldiers at the foot of a kopje. He crept cautiously around the kopje, and, when he was within a hundred yards of the men, he shouted, "Hands up!" The soldiers immediately lifted their arms, and, in obedience to the orders of Marks, stacked their guns on a rock and advanced toward him. Marks placed the men in a line, saw that there were twenty-three big, able-bodied soldiers, and then marched them back into camp, to the great astonishment of his generals and fellow burghers.

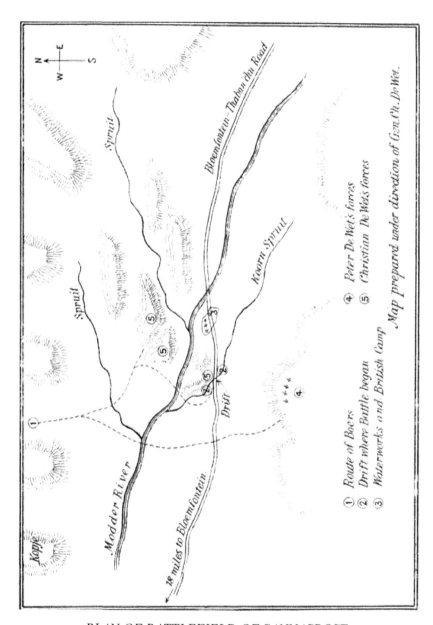

PLAN OF BATTLEFIELD OF SANNASPOST

6. The Boers in Battle

The battle of Sannaspost on March 31st was one of the few engagements in the campaign in which the forces of the Boers and the British were almost numerically equal. There were two or three small battles in which the Boers had more men engaged than the British, but in the majority of instances the Boers were vastly outnumbered both in men and guns. At Elandslaagte the Boers had exactly seven hundred and fifty burghers pitted against the five or six thousand British; Spion Kop was won from three thousand British by three hundred and fifty Boers; at the Tugela Botha with not more than twenty-six hundred men fought for more than a week against ten times that number of soldiers under General Buller; while the greatest disparity between the opposing forces was at Paardeberg, where Cronje spent a week in trying to lead his four thousand men through the encircling wall of forty or fifty thousand British soldiers.

Sannaspost was not a decisive battle of the war, since no point of great strategical importance was at stake, but it was more in the nature of a demonstration of what the Boers were able to do when they were opposed to a force of equal strength. It was a test which was equally fair to both contestants, and neither of them could reasonably claim to have possessed an advantage over the other a day before the battle was fought. The British commander, Colonel Broadwood, had seventeen hundred men in his column, and General De Wet was at the head of about two hundred and fifty less than that number, but the strength of the forces was equalised by the Boer general's intimate knowledge of the country. Colonel Broadwood was experienced in Indian, Egyptian, and South

African warfare, and the majority of his soldiers were seasoned in many battles. De Wet and his men were fresh from Poplar Grove, Abraham's Kraal, and the fighting around Kimberley, but they were not better nor worse than the average of the Boer burghers. The British commander was hampered by a large transport train, but he possessed the advantage of more heavy guns than his adversary. All in all, the two forces were equally matched when they reached the battlefield.

The day before the battle General De Wet and his men were in laager several miles east of Brandfort, whither they had fled after the fall of Bloemfontein. His scouts brought to him the information that a small British column was stationed in the village of Thaba N'Chu, forty miles to the east, and he determined to march thither and attack it. He gave the order, "Opzaal!" and in less than eight minutes every one of his burghers was on his horse, armed, provided with two days' rations of biltong, biscuit, coffee, and sugar, and ready to proceed. De Wet himself leaped into a light, ramshackle four-wheeler, and led the advance over the dusty veld. Without attempting to proceed with any semblance of military order, the burghers followed in the course of their leader, some riding rapidly, others walking beside their horses, and a few skirmishing far away on the veld for buck. The mule-teams dragging the artillery and the ammunition wagons were not permitted by their hullabalooing Basuto drivers to lag far behind the general, and the dust which was raised by this long cavalcade was not unlike the clouds of locusts which were frequently mistaken for the signs of a trekking commando. Mile after mile was rapidly traversed, until darkness came on, when a halt was made so that the burghers might prepare a meal, and that the general might hear from the scouts, who were far in advance of the body. After the men and horses had eaten, and the moon rose over the dark peak of Thaba N'Chu mountain, the burghers lighted their pipes and sang psalms and hymns until the peaceful valley resounded with their voices.

Panting horses brought to the little stone farmhouse, where General De Wet was drinking milk, the long-awaited scouts who carried the information that the British force had evacuated Thaba N'Chu late in the afternoon, and that it was moving hurriedly toward Bloemfontein. Again the order: "Opzaal," and the mule train came into motion and the burghers mounted their horses. A chill night air arose, and shivering burghers wrapped blankets around their shoulders. The humming of hymns and the whistling ceased, and there was nothing but the clatter of horses' hoofs, the shouts of the Basutos, and the noises of the guns and wagons rumbling over the stones and gullies to mark the nocturnal passage of the army. Lights appeared at farmhouse windows, and at their gates were women and children with bread and bowls of milk and prayers for the burghers. Small walls enclosing family burial plots where newly-dug ground told its own story of the war seemed grim in the moonlight; native huts with their inhabitants standing like spectres before the doors appeared like monstrous ant-heaps--all these were passed, but the drooping eyes of the burghers saw nothing. At midnight another halt was made, horses were off-saddled and men lay down on the veld to sleep. The generals and officers met in Krijgsraad, and other scouts arriving told of the enemy's evident intention of spending the remainder of the night at an old-time off-saddling station known as Sannaspost. The news was highly important, and the heads of the generals came closer together. Maps were produced, pencil marks were made, plans were formed, and then the sleeping burghers were aroused. The trek was resumed, and shortly afterward the column was divided into two parts; the one consisting of nine hundred men under General Peter De Wet, proceeding by a circuitous route to the hills south of Sannaspost, and the other of five hundred men commanded by General Christian De Wet moving through a maze of kopjes to a position west of the trekking station.

VILLAGE AND MOUNTAIN OF THABA N'CHU

The burghers were not informed of the imminence of a battle; but they required no such announcement from their generals. The atmosphere seemed to be surcharged with premonitions of an engagement, and men rubbed sleep out of their eyes and sat erect upon their horses. The blacks even ceased to crack their whips so sharply, and urged the mules forward in whispers instead of shrieks. Burghers took their rifles from their backs, tested the workings of the mechanism and filled the magazine with cartridges. Artillerymen leaped from their horses and led them while they sat on the cannon and poured oil into the bearings. Young men speculated on the number of prisoners they would take; old men wrote their names on their hats by the light of the moon. The lights of Bloemfontein appeared in the distance, and grey-beards looked longingly at them and sighed. But the cavalcade passed on, grimly, silently, and defiantly, into the haunts of the enemy.

After four hours of trekking over veld, kopje, sloot, and donga, the two columns halted, the burghers dismounted, and, weary from the long journey and the lack of sleep, lay down on the earth beside their horses. Commandants, field-cornets and corporals, bustling about among the burghers, horses and wagons, gave orders in undertones; generals summoned their scouts and asked for detailed information concerning the whereabouts of the enemy; patrols were scurrying hither and thither to secure accurate ideas of the topography of the territory in front of them; all who were in authority were busy, while the burghers, who carried the strength of battle in their bodies, lay sleeping and resting.

The first dim rays of the day came over the tops of the eastern hills when the burghers were aroused and asked to proceed to the positions chosen by their leaders. The men under Peter De Wet, the younger brother of the Commandant-General, were led to an elevation about a mile and a half south of Sannaspost, where they placed their cannon into position and waited for the break of day.

Christian De Wet and his five hundred burghers advanced noiselessly and occupied the dry bed of Koorn Spruit, a stream which crossed the main road running from Thaba N'Chu to Bloemfontein at right angles about a mile from the station where the British forces had begun their bivouac for the night, two hours before. No signs of the enemy could be seen; there were no pickets, no outposts, and none of the usual safeguards of an army, and for some time the Boers were led to believe that the British force had been allowed to escape unharmed.

The burghers under the leadership of Christian De Wet were completely concealed in the spruit. The high banks might have been held by the forces of their enemy, but unless they crept to the edge and looked down into the stream they would not have been able to discover the presence of the Boers. Where the road crossed the stream deep approaches had been dug into the banks in order to facilitate the passage of conveyances--a "drift" it is called in South Africa--and on either side for a distance of a mile, up and down the stream, the burghers stood by their horses and waited for the coming of the day. The concealment was perfect; no specially constructed trenches could have served the purposes of the Boers more advantageously.

Dawn lighted the flat-topped kopjes that lay in a huge semicircle in the distance, and men clambered up the sides of the spruit to ascertain the camp of the enemy. The white smoke-stack of the Bloemfontein waterworks appeared against the black background of the hills in the east, but it was still too dark to distinguish objects on the ground beneath it. A group of burghers in the spruit, absent-mindedly, began to sing a deep-toned psalm, but the stern order of a commandant quickly ended their matutinal song. A donkey in an ammunition wagon brayed vociferously, and a dozen men, fearful lest the enemy should hear the noise, sprang upon him with clubs and whips, and even attempted to close his mouth by force of hands. It was the fateful moment before the battle, and men acted strangely. Some walked nervously up and down, others dropped on their knees and prayed, a few lighted their pipes, many sat on the ground and looked vacantly into space, while some of the younger burghers joked and laughed.

At the drift stood the generals, scanning the hills and undulations with their glasses. Small fires appeared in the east near the tall white stack. "They are preparing their breakfast," some one suggested. "I see a few tents," another one reported excitedly. All eyes were turned in the direction indicated. Some estimated the intervening distance at a mile, others were positive it was not more than a thousand yards--it was not light enough to distinguish accurately. "Tell the burghers that I will fire the first shot," said General De Wet to one of his staff. Immediately the order was spread to the men in the spruit. "I see men leading oxen to the wagons; they are preparing to trek," remarked a commandant. "They are coming down this way," announced another, slapping his thigh joyfully.

A few minutes afterwards clouds of dust arose, and at intervals the wagons in the van could be seen coming down the slope toward the drift. The few tents fell, and men in brown uniforms moved hither and thither near the waterworks building. Wagon after wagon joined in the procession; drivers were shrieking and wielding their whips over the heads of the oxen, and farther behind were cavalrymen mounting their horses. It was daylight then, although the sun was still below the horizon, and the movements of the enemy could be plainly discerned. The ox-teams came slowly down the road--there seemed to be no limit to their number--and the generals retreated down the drift to the bottom of the spruit, so that their presence should not be discerned by the enemy, and to await the arrival of the wagons.

The shrieking natives drew nearer, the rumbling of the wagons became more distinct, and soon the first vehicle descended the drift. A few burghers were sent forward to intercept it. As soon as it reached the bottom of the spruit the men grasped the bridles of the horses, and instantly there were shrieks from the occupants of the vehicle. It was filled with women and children, all pale with fright on account of the unexpected appearance of the Boers. The passengers were quickly and gently taken from the wagon and sent to places of safety in the spruit, while a burgher jumped into the vehicle and drove the horses up the other drift and out upon the open veld. The operation of substituting drivers was done so quickly and quietly that none of those approaching the drift from the other side noticed anything extraordinary, and proceeded into the spruit. Other burghers stood prepared to receive them as they descended the drift with their heavily laden ammunition and provision wagons, and there was little trouble in seizing the British drivers and placing the whips into the hands of Boers. Wagon after wagon was relieved of its drivers and sent up to the other bank without creating a suspicion in the minds of the others who were coming down the slope from the waterworks.

After fifty or more wagons had crossed the drift a solitary cavalry officer with the rank of captain, riding leisurely along, followed one of them. His coat had a rent in it and he was holding the torn parts together, as if he were planning the mending of it when he reached Bloemfontein. A young Boer sprang toward him, called "Hands up!" and projected the barrel of his carbine toward him. The officer started out of his reverie, involuntarily reached for his sword, but repented almost instantly, and obeyed the order. General De Wet approached the captain, touched his hat in salute, and said, "Good morning, sir." The officer returned the complimentary greeting and offered his sword to the Boer. De Wet declined to receive the weapon and told the officer to return to his men and ask them to surrender. "We have a large force of men surrounding you," the general explained, "and you cannot escape. In order to save many lives I ask you to surrender your men without fighting." The officer remained silent for a moment, then looked squarely into the eyes of the Boer general and said, "I will return to my men and will order them to surrender." De Wet nodded his head in assent, and the captain mounted his horse. "I will rely upon your promise," the general added, "if you break it I will shoot you."

General De Wet and several of his commandants followed the cavalry officer up the drift and stood on the bank while the horseman galloped slowly toward the troops which were following the wagons down the slope. The general raised his carbine and held it in his arms. His eyes were fixed on the officer, and he stood as firm as a statue until the cavalryman reached his men. There was a momentary pause while the captain stood before his troops, then the horses were wheeled about and their hoofs sent showers of dust into the air as they carried their riders in retreat. General De Wet stepped forward several paces, raised his carbine to his shoulder, aimed steadily for a second, then fired. The bullet whistled menacingly over the heads of oxen and drivers--it struck the officer, and he fell.[1]

All along the banks of the spruit, for a mile on either side of the ravine, and over on the hills where Peter De Wet and his burghers lay, men had been waiting patiently and expectantly for that signal gun of Christian De Wet. They had been watching the enemy toiling down the slope under the very muzzles of their guns for almost an age, it seemed, yet they dared not fire lest the plans of the generals should be thwarted. Men had lain flat on the ground with their rifles pointing minute after minute at individuals in the advancing column, but the words of their general, "I will fire the first shot," restrained them. The flight of the bullet which entered the body of the cavalry officer marked the ending of the long period of nervous tension, and the burghers were free to use their guns.

Until the officer advised his men to retreat and he himself fell from his horse the main body of the British troops was ignorant of the presence of the Boers, but the report of the rifle was a summons to battle and instantly the field was filled with myriads of stirring scenes. The lazy transport-train suddenly became a thing of rapid motion; the huge body of troops was quickly broken into many parts; horses that had been idling along the road plunged forward as if projected by catapults. Officers with swords flashing in the sunlight appeared leading their men into different positions, cannon were hurriedly drawn upon commanding elevations, and Red Cross wagons scattered to places of safety. The peaceful transport-train had suddenly been transformed into a formidable engine of war by the report of a rifle, and the contest for a sentiment and a bit of ground was opened by shrieking cannon-shell and the piercing cry of rifle-ball.

Down at the foot of the slope, where the drift crossed the spruit, Boers were dragging cannon into position, and in among the wagons which had become congested in the road, burghers and soldiers were engaging in fierce hand-to-hand encounters. A stocky Briton wrestled with a youthful Boer, and in the struggle both fell to the ground; near by a cavalryman was firing his revolver at a Boer armed with a rifle, and a hundred paces away a burgher was fighting with a

---

[1] *This incident of the battle was witnessed by the writer, as well as by several of the foreign military attachés. Whether the British officer broke his promise by asking his men to retreat or whether his troopers were disobedient is a question, but it is more than likely that he endeavoured to act in good faith. Whether the officer was killed or only wounded by General De Wet's shot could not be ascertained.*

British officer for the possession of a sword. Over from the hills in the south came the dull roar of Boer cannon, followed by the reports of the shells exploding in the east near the waterworks. British cannon opened fire from a position near the white smoke-stack and scores of bursting projectiles fell among the wagons at the spruit. Oxen and horses were rent limb from limb, wagons tumbled over on their sides; boxes of provisions were thrown in all directions, and out of the cloud of dust and smoke stumbled men with blood-stained faces and lacerated bodies. Terrified and bellowing oxen twisted and tugged at their yokes; horses broke from their fastenings in the wagons and dashed hither and thither, and weakling donkeys strove in vain to free themselves from wagons set on fire by the shells. Explosion followed explosion, and with every one the mass became more entangled. Dead horses fell upon living oxen; wheels and axles were thrown on the backs of donkeys, and plunging mules dragged heavy wagons over great piles of *débris*.

THE AUTHOR, AND A BASUTO PONY WHICH ASSISTED IN THE
FIGHT AT SANNASPOST

The cannon on the southern hills became more active and their shells caused the landscape surrounding the waterworks to be filled with geysers of dust. Troops which were stationed near the white smoke-stack suddenly spurred their horses forward and dashed northward to seek safety behind a long undulation in the ground. The artillerymen in the hills followed their movements with shells, and the dust-fountains sprang up at the very heels of the troops. The cannon at the drift joined in the attack on the horsemen scattered over the slope, and the big guns at the waterworks continued to reply vigorously. The men in the spruit were watching the artillery duel intently as they sped up and down the bottom of the water-less stream, searching for points of vantage. A large number of them moved rapidly down the spruit towards its confluence with the Modder River in order to check the advance of the troops driven forward by the shell-fire, and another party rushed eastward to secure positions in the rear of the British cannon at the waterworks. The banks of the stream still concealed them, but they dared not fire lest the enemy should disturb their plans. On and on they dashed, over rocks and chasms, until they were within a few hundred yards of a part of the British force. Slowly they crept up the sides of the spruit, cautiously peered out over the edge of the bank and then opened fire on the men at the cannon and the troops passing down the slope. Little jets of dust arose where their bullets struck the ground, men fell around the cannon, and cavalrymen quickly turned and charged toward the spruit. The shells of the cannon at the drift and on the southern hills fell thicker and thicker among the troops and the air above them was heavy with the light blue smoke of bursting shrapnel. The patter of the Boer rifles at the spruit increased in intensity and the jets of brown dust became more numerous. The cavalrymen leaped from their horses and ran ahead to find protection behind a line of rocks. The intermittent, irregular firing of the Boers was punctuated by the regular, steady reports of British volleys. The brown dust-geysers increased among the rocks where the British lay, and soon the soldiers turned and ran for their horses. Burghers crept from rock to rock in pursuit of them, and their bullets urged the fleeing horsemen on. The British cannon spoke less frequently, and shells and bullets fell so thickly around them that bravery in such a situation seemed suicidal, and the last artilleryman fled. Boers ran up and turned the loaded guns upon the backs of those who had operated them a few moments before.

Down in the north-western part of the field a large force of troops was dashing over the veld toward the banks of the spruit. Officers, waving swords above their heads and shouting commands to their subordinates, led the way. A few shells exploding in the ranks scattered the force temporarily and caused horses to rear and plunge, but the gaps quickly disappeared, and the men moved on down the slope. Boers rode rapidly down the spruit and out upon the veld behind a low range of kopjes which lay in front of the British force. Horses were left in charge of native servants, and the burghers crept forward on hands and knees to the summit of the range. They carefully concealed themselves behind rocks and bushes and waited for the enemy to approach more closely. The cavalrymen spread out in skirmishing order as they proceeded, and, ignorant of the proximity of the Boers, drew their horses into a walk. The burghers in the kopje fired a few shots, and the troops turned quickly to the left and again broke into a gallop. The firing from the kopje increased in volume, the cannon from the hills again broke forth, the little dust-clouds rose out of the earth on all sides of the troopers, and shrapnel bursting in the air sent its bolts and balls of iron and steel; into the midst of the brown men and earth. Horses and riders fell, officers leaped to the ground and shouted encouragement to their soldiers, men sprang behind rocks and discharged their rifles. Minutes of agony passed. Officers gathered their men and attempted to lead them forward, but they had not progressed far when the Boers in the spruit in front of them swept the ground with the bullets of their rifles. Burghers crept around the edge of the kopjes and emptied their carbines into the backs of the cavalrymen, cannons poured shell upon them from three different directions, and these men on the open plain could not see even a brace of Boers to fire upon. Men and horses continued to fall, the wounded lay moaning in the grass, while shells and bullets sang their song of death more loudly every second to those who braved the storm. A tiny white cloth was raised, the firing ceased instantly, and the brave band threw down its arms to the burghers who sprang out from the spruit and rocky kopje.

In the east the low hills were dotted with men in brown. To the right and left of them, a thousand yards apart, were Boer horsemen circling around kopjes and seeking positions for attacking the already vanquished but stubborn enemy. Rifle fire had ceased and cannon sounded only at intervals of a few minutes. Women at the doors of the two farmhouses in the centre of the battlefield, and a man drawing water at a well near by, were not inharmonious with the quietness and calmness of the moment, but the epoch of peace was of short duration. The Boer horsemen stemmed the retreat of the men in brown, and compelled them to retrace their steps. Another body of burghers made a wide *détour* north-eastward from the spruit, and, jumping from their horses, crept along under the cover of an undulation in the ground for almost a half-mile to a point which overlooked the route of the British retreat.

The enemy was slow in coming, and a few of the Boers lay down to sleep. Others filled their pipes and lighted them, and one abstracted a pebble from his shoe. As the cavalrymen drew nearer to them the burghers crept forward several paces and sought the protection of rocks or piled stones together in the form of miniature forts. "Shall we fire now?" inquired a beardless Free State youth. "Wait until they come nearer," replied an older burgher close by. Silence was maintained for several minutes, when the youth again became uneasy. "I can hit the first one of those Lancers," he begged, as he pointed with his carbine to a cavalryman known to the Boers as a "Lancer," whether he carried a lance or not. The cannon in the south urged the cavalrymen forward with a few shells delivered a short distance behind them, and then the old burgher called to the youth, "See if you can hit him now."

The boy missed the rider but killed the horse, and the British force quickly dismounted and sought shelter in a small ravine. The reports of volley firing followed, and bullets cut the grass beside the burghers and flattened themselves against the rocks. Another volley, and a third, in rapid succession, and the burghers pressed more closely to the ground. An interval of a minute, and they glanced over their tiny stockades to find a British soldier. "They are coming up the kopje!" shouted a burgher, and their rifles swept the hillside with bullets. More volleys came from below and, while the leaden tongues sang above and around them, the burghers turned and lay on their backs to refill the magazines of their rifles. Another interval, and the attack was renewed. "They are running!" screamed a youth exultingly, and burghers rose and fired at the men in brown at the foot of the kopje. Marksmen had their opportunity then, and long aim was taken before a shot was fired. Men knelt on the one knee and rested an elbow on the other, while they held their rifles to their shoulders. Reports of carbines became less frequent as the troops progressed farther in an opposite direction, but increased again when the cavalrymen returned for a second attack upon the kopje. "Lend me a handful of cartridges, Jan," asked one man of his neighbour, as they watched the oncoming force.

"They must want this kopje," remarked another burgher jocularly, as he filled his pipe with tobacco and lighted it.

The British cannon in the east again became active, and the dust raised by their shells was blown over the heads of the burghers on the kopje. The reports of the big guns of the Boers reverberated among the hills, while the regular volleys of the British rifles seemed to be beating time to the minor notes and irregular reports of the Boer carbines. At a distance the troops moving over the brown field of battle resembled huge ants more than human beings; and the use of smokeless powder, causing the panorama to remain perfectly clear and distinct, allowed every movement to be closely followed by the observer. Cannon poured forth their tons of shells, but there was nothing except the sound of the explosion to denote where the guns were situated. Rifles cut down lines of men, but there was no smoke to indicate where they were being operated, and unless the burghers or soldiers displayed themselves to their enemy there was nothing to indicate their positions. Shrapnel bursting in the air, the reports of rifles and heavy guns and the little puffs of dust where shells and bullets struck the ground were the only evidences of the battle's progress. The hand-to-hand conflicts, the duels with bayonets and swords and the clouds of smoke were probably heroic and picturesque before the age of rapid-fire guns, modern rifles, and smokeless ammunition, but here the field of battle resembled a country fox-chase with an exaggerated number of hunters, more than a representation of a battle of twenty-five years ago.

On the summit of the kopje the burghers were firing leisurely but accurately. One man aimed steadily at a soldier for fully twenty seconds, then pressed the trigger, lowered his rifle and watched for the effect of the shot. Bullets were flying high over him, and the shrapnel of the enemy's guns exploded far behind him. There seemed to be no great danger, and he fired again. "I missed that time," he remarked to a burgher who lay behind another rock several yards distant. His neighbour then fired at the same soldier, and both cried simultaneously: "He is hit!" The enemy again disappeared in the little ravine, and the burghers ceased firing. Shells continued to tear through the air, but none exploded in the vicinity of the men, and they took advantage of the lull in the battle to light their pipes. A swarm of yellow locusts passed overhead, and exploding shrapnel tore them into myriads of pieces, their wings and limbs falling near the burghers. "I am glad I am not a locust," remarked a burgher farther to the left of the others, as he dropped a handful of torn fragments of the insects. Shells and bullets suddenly splashed everywhere around the burghers, and they crouched more closely behind the rocks. The enemy's guns had secured an accurate range, and the air was filled with the projectiles of iron and lead. Exploding shells splintered rocks into atoms and sent them tearing through the grass. Puffs of smoke and dirt were springing up from every square yard of ground, and a few men rose from their retreats and ran to the rear where the Basuto servants were holding their horses. More followed several minutes afterwards, and when those who remained on the summit of the kopje saw that ten times their number of soldiers were ascending the hill under cover of cannon fire they also fled to their horses.

An open plain half a mile wide lay between the point where the burghers mounted their horses, and another kopje in the north-east. The men lay closely on their horses' backs, plunged their spurs in the animals' sides, and dashed forward. The cavalrymen, who had gained the summit of the kopje meanwhile, opened fire on the fleeing Boers, and their bullets cut open the horses' sides and ploughed holes into the burgher's clothing. One horse, a magnificent grey who had been leading the others, fell dead as he was leaping over a small gully, and his rider was thrown headlong to the ground. Another horseman turned in his course, assisted the horseless rider to his own brown steed, and the two were borne rapidly through the storm of bullets towards the kopje. Another horse was killed when he had carried his rider almost to the goal of safety, and the Boer was compelled to traverse the remainder of the distance on foot. Apparently all the burghers had escaped across the plain, and their field-cornet was preparing to lead them to another position when a solitary horseman, a mere speck of black against a background of brown, lifeless grass, issued from a rocky ravine below the kopje occupied by the enemy, and plunged into the open space. Lee-Metfords cracked and cut open the ground around him, but the rider bent forward and seemed to become a part of his horse. Every rod of progress seemed to multiply the fountains of dust near him; every leap of his horse seemed necessarily his last. On, on he dashed, now using his stirrups, now beating his horse with his hands. It seemed as if he were making no progress, yet his horse's legs were moving so swiftly. "They will get him," sighed the field-cornet, looking through his glasses. "He has a chance," replied a burgher. Seconds dragged wearily, the firing increased in volume, and the dust of the horse's heels mingled with that raised by the bullets. The sound of the hoofs beating down on the solid earth came louder and louder over the veld, the firing slackened and then ceased, and a foaming, panting horse brought his burden to where the burghers stood. The exhausted rider sank to the ground, and men patted the neck and forehead of the quivering beast.

Down in the valley, near the spruit, the foreign military attachés in uniforms quite distinct were watching the effect of the British artillery on the saddle belonging to one of their number. "They will never hit it," volunteered one, as a shell exploded ten yards distant from the leathern mark.

"They must think it is a crowd of Boers," suggested another, when a dozen shells had fallen without injuring the saddle. Fifteen, twenty tongues of dust arose, but the leather remained unmarred by scratch or rent, and the attachés became the target of the heavy guns. "I am hit," groaned Lieutenant Nix, of the Netherlands-Indian army, and his companions caught him in their arms. Blood gushed from a wound in the shoulder, but the soldier spirit did not desert him. "Here, Demange!" he called to the French attaché, "Hold my head. And you, Thompson and Allen, see if you cannot bind this shoulder." The Norwegian and Hollander bound the wound as well as they were able. "Reichman!" the injured man whispered, "I am going to die in a few minutes, and I wish you would write a letter to my wife." The American attaché hastily procured paper and pencil, and while shells and shrapnel were bursting over and around them the wounded man dictated a letter to his wife in Holland. Blood flowed copiously from the wound and stained the grass upon which he lay. He was pale as the clouds above him, and the pain was agonising, but the dying man's letter was filled with nothing but expressions of love and tenderness.

In the south-eastern part of the field a large party of cavalrymen was speeding in the direction of Thaba N'Chu. On two sides of them, a thousand yards behind, small groups of horsemen were giving chase. At a distance, the riders appeared like ants slowly climbing the hillside. Now and then a Boer rider suddenly stopped his horse, leaped to the ground, and fired at the fleeing cavalrymen. A second afterwards he was on his horse again, bending to the chase. Shot followed shot, but the distance between the forces grew greater, and one by one the burghers turned their animals' heads and slowly retraced their steps. A startled buck bounded over the veld, two rifles were turned upon it, and its flight was ended.

CALLING FOR VOLUNTEERS TO MAN CAPTURED CANNON AFTER SANNASPOST

The sound of firing had ceased, and the battle was concluded. Wagons with Red Cross flags fluttering from the tall staffs above them, issued from the mountains and rumbled through the valleys. Burghers dashed over the field in search of the wounded and dying. Men who a few moments before were straining every nerve to kill their fellow-beings became equally energetic to preserve lives. Wounded soldiers and burghers were lifted out of the grass and carried tenderly to the ambulance wagons. The dead were placed side by side, and the same cloth covered the bodies of Boer and Briton. Men with spades upturned the earth, and stood grimly by while a man in black prayed over the bodies of those who died for their country.

Boer officers, with pencils and paper in their hands, sped over the battlefield from a group of prisoners to a line of passing wagons, and made calculations concerning the result of the day's battle. Three Boers killed and nine wounded was one side of the account. On the credit sheet were marked four hundred and eight British soldiers, seven cannon, one hundred and fifty wagons, five hundred and fifty rifles, two thousand horses and cattle, and vast stores of ammunition and provisions captured during the day.

In among the north-eastern hills, where a farmer's daub-and-wattle cottage stood, were the prisoners of war, chatting and joking with their captors. The officers walked slowly back and forth, never raising their eyes from the ground. Dejection was written on their faces. Near them were the captured wagons, with groups of noisy soldiers climbing over them in search of their luggage. On the ground others were playing cards and matching coins. Young Boers walked amongst them and engaged them in conversation. Near the farmhouse stood a tall Cape Colony Boer talking with his former neighbour, who was a prisoner. Several Americans among the captured disputed the merits of the war with a Yankee burgher, who had readily distinguished his countrymen among the throng. Some one began to whistle a popular tune, others joined, and soon almost every one was participating. An officer gave the order for the prisoners to fall in line, and shortly afterward the men in brown tramped forward, while the burghers stepped aside and lined the path. A soldier commenced to sing another popular song, British and Boer caught the refrain, and the noise of tramping feet was drowned by the melody of the united voices of friend and foe singing--

"It's the soldiers of the Queen, my lads, Who've been, my lads--who've seen, my lads, * * * * * We'll proudly point to every one Of England's soldiers of the Queen."

7. The Generals of the War

The names and deeds of the men who led thirty thousand of their fellow-peasants against almost a quarter of a million of the trained troops of the greatest empire in the world, and husbanded their men and resources so that they were enabled to continue the unequal struggle for the greater part of a year will live for ever in the history of the Dark Continent. When racial hatred and the bitternesses of the war have been forgotten, and South Africa has emerged from its long period of bloodshed and disaster, then all Afrikanders will revere the memory of the valiant deeds of Cronje, Joubert, Botha, Meyer, De Wet, and the others who fought so gallantly in a cause which they considered just and holy. Such noble examples of heroism as Cronje's stand at Paardeberg, Botha's defence of the Tugela and the region east of Pretoria; De Wet's warfare in the Free State, and Meyer's fighting in the Transvaal will shine in African history as long as the Southern Cross illumes the path of civilised people in that region. When future generations search the pages of history for deeds of valour they will turn to the records of the Boer-British war of 1899-1900, and find that the military leaders of the farmers of South Africa were not less valorous than those of the untrained followers of Cromwell or William of Orange, the peace-loving mountaineers of Switzerland, or the patriotic countrymen of Washington.

The leaders of the Boer forces were not generals in the popular sense of the word. Almost without exception, they were men who had no technical knowledge of warfare; men who were utterly without military training of any nature, and who would have been unable to pass an examination for the rank of corporal in a European army. Among the entire list of generals who fought in the armies of the two Republics there were not more than three who had ever read military works, and Cronje was the only one who ever studied the theory and practice of modern warfare, and made an attempt to apply the principles of it to his army. Every one of the Boer generals was a farmer who, before the war, paid more attention to his crops and cattle than he did to evolving ideas for application in a campaign, and the majority of them, in fact, never dreamed that they would be called upon to be military leaders until they were nominated for the positions a short time before hostilities were commenced. Joubert, Cronje, Ferreira, and Meyer were about the only men in the two Republics who were certain that they would be called upon to lead their countrymen, for all had had experience in former wars; but men like Botha, De Wet, De la Rey, and Snyman, who occupied responsible positions afterward, had no such assurance, and naturally gave little or no attention to the study of military matters. The men who became the Boer generals gained their military knowledge in the wilds and on the veld of South Africa where they were able to develop their natural genius in the hunting of lions and the tracking of game. The Boer principle of hunting was precisely the same as their method of warfare and consequently the man who, in times of peace, was a successful leader of shooting expeditions was none the less adept afterward as the leader of commandos.

When the Volksraad of the Transvaal determined to send an ultimatum to Great Britain, it was with the knowledge that such an act would provoke war, and consequently preparations for hostilities were immediately made. One of the first acts was the appointment of five assistant commandant-generals--Piet Cronje, Schalk Burgher, Lucas Meyer, Daniel Erasmus, and Jan Kock--all of whom held high positions in the Government, and were respected by the Boer people. After hostilities commenced, and it became necessary to have more generals, six other names were added to the list of assistants of Commandant-General Joubert--those chosen being Sarel Du Toit, Hendrik Schoeman, John De la Rey, Hendrik Snyman, and Herman R. Lemmer. The selections which were so promiscuously made were proved by time to be wise, for almost without exception the men developed into extraordinarily capable generals. In the early part of the campaign many costly mistakes and errors of judgment were made by some of the newly-appointed generals, but such misfortunes were only to be expected from men who suddenly found themselves face to face with some of the best-trained generals in the world. Later, when the campaign had been in progress for several months, and the farmers had had opportunities of learning the tactics of their opponents, they made no move unless they were reasonably certain of the result.

One of the prime reasons for the great success which attended the Boer army before the strength of the enemy's forces became overwhelming, was the fact that the generals were allowed to operate in parts of the country with which they were thoroughly acquainted. General Cronje operated along the western frontiers of the Republics, where he knew the geographical features of the country as well as he did those of his own farm. General Meyer spent the greater part of his life in the neighbourhood of the Biggarsberg and northern Natal, and there was hardly a rod of that territory with which he was unfamiliar. General Botha was born near the Tugela, and, in his boyhood days, pursued the buck where afterward he made such a brave resistance against the forces of General Buller. General Christian De Wet was a native of Dewetsdorp, and there was not a sloot or donga in all the territory where he fought so valiantly that he had not traversed scores of times before the war began. General De la Rey spent the greater part of his life in Griqualand West, Cape Colony, and when he was leading his men around Kimberley and the south-western part of the Free State he was in familiar territory. General Snyman, who besieged Mafeking, was a resident of the Marico district, and consequently was acquainted with the formation of the country in the western part of the Transvaal. In the majority of cases the generals did not need the services of an intelligence department, except to determine the whereabouts of the enemy, for no scouts or patrols could furnish a better account of the nature of the country in which they were fighting than that which existed in the minds of the leaders. Under these conditions there was not the slightest chance for any of the generals falling into a trap laid by the enemy, but there always were opportunities for leading the enemy into ambush.

The Boer generals also had the advantage of having excellent maps of the country in which they were fighting, and by means of these they were enabled to explain proposed movements to the commandants and field-cornets who were not familiar with the topography of the land. These maps were made two years before the war by a corps of experts employed by the Transvaal Government, and on them was a representation of every foot of ground in the Transvaal, Free State, Natal, and Cape Colony. A small elevation near Durban and a spruit near Cape Town were marked as plainly as a kopje near Pretoria, while the British forts at Durban and Cape Town were as accurately pictured as the roads that led to them. The Boers had a map of the environs of Ladysmith which was a hundred times better than that furnished by the British War Office, yet Ladysmith was the Natal base of the British army for many years.

The greater part of the credit for the Boers' preparedness must be given to the late Commandant-General Piet J. Joubert, who was the head of the Transvaal War Department for many years. General Joubert, or "Old Piet," as he was called by the Boers, to distinguish him from the many other Jouberts in the country, was undoubtedly a great military leader in his younger days, but he was almost seventy years old when he was called upon to lead his people against the army of Great Britain, and at that age very few men are capable of great mental or physical exertion. There was no greater patriot in the Transvaal than he, and no one who desired the absolute independence of his country more sincerely than the old general; yet his heart was not in the fighting. Like Kruger, he was a man of peace, and to his dying day he believed that the war might have been avoided easily. Unlike Kruger, he clung to the idea that the war, having been forced upon them, should be ended as speedily as possible, and without regard to the loss of national interests. Joubert valued the lives of the burghers more highly than a clause in a treaty, and rather than see his countrymen slain in battle he was willing to make concessions to those who harassed his Government.

Joubert was one of the few public men in the Transvaal who firmly believed that the differences between the two countries would be amicably adjusted, and he constantly opposed the measures for arming the country which were brought before him. The large armament was secured by him, it is true, but the Volksraads compelled him to purchase the arms and ammunition. If Joubert had been a man who loved war he would have secured three times as great a quantity of war material as there was in the country when the war was begun; but he was distinctly a man who loved peace. He constantly allowed his sentiments to overrule his judgment of what was good for his country, and the result of that line of action was that at the beginning of hostilities there were more Boer guns in Europe and on the ocean than there were in the Transvaal.

General Joubert was a grand old Boer in many respects, and no better, more righteous, and more upright man ever lived. He worked long and faithfully for his people, and he undoubtedly strove to do that which he believed to be the best for his country, but he was incapable of performing the duties of his office as a younger, more energetic, and a more warlike man would have attended to them. Joubert was in his dotage, and none of his people were aware of it until the crucial moment of the war was passed. When he led the Boers at Majuba and Laing's Nek, in 1881, he was in the prime of his life--energetic, resourceful, and undaunted by any reverses. In 1899, when he followed the commandos into Natal, he was absolutely the reverse--slow, wavering, and too timid to move from his tent. He constantly remained many miles in the rear of the advance column, and only once went into the danger zone, when he led a small com- mando south of the Tugela. Then, instead of leading his victorious burghers against the forces of the enemy, he retreated precipitately at the first sign of danger, and established himself at Modderspruit, a day's journey from the foremost commandos, where he remained with almost ten thousand of his men for three months.

Joubert attempted to wage war without the shedding of blood, and he failed. When General Meyer reported that about thirty Boers had been killed and injured in the fight at Dundee, the Commandant-General censured him harshly for making such a great sacrifice of blood, and forbade him from following the fleeing enemy, as such a course would entail still greater casualties. When Sir George White and his forces had been imprisoned in Ladysmith, and there was almost a clear path to Durban, Joubert held back and would not risk the lives of a few hundred burghers, even when it was pointed out to him that the men themselves were eager to assume the responsibility. He made only one effort to capture Ladysmith, but the slight loss of life so appalled him that he would never sanction another attack, although the town could easily have been taken on the following day if an attempt had been made. Although he had a large army round the besieged town he did not dig a yard of entrenchment in all the time he was at Modderspruit, nor would he hearken to any plans for capturing the starving garrison by means of progressive trenches. While Generals Botha, Meyer, and Erasmus, with less than three thousand men, were holding the enemy at the Tugela, Joubert, with three times that number of men to guard impotent Ladysmith, declined to send any ammunition for their big guns, voted to retreat, and finally fled northward to Colenso, deserting the fighting men, destroying the bridges and railways as he progressed, and even leaving his own tents and equipment behind.

There were extenuating circumstances in connection with Joubert's failure in the campaign--his age, an illness, and an accident while he was in laager--and it is but charitable to grant that these were fundamentally responsible for his shortcomings, but it is undoubted that he was primarily responsible for the failure of the Natal campaign. The army which he commanded in Natal, although only twelve or thirteen thousand men in strength, was the equal in fighting ability of seventy-five thousand British troops, and the only thing it lacked was a man who would fight with them and lead them after a fleeing enemy. If the Commandant-General had pursued the British forces after all their defeats and had drawn the burghers out of their laagers by the force of his own example, the major part of the history of the Natal campaign would have been made near the Indian Ocean instead of on the banks of the Tugela. The majority of the Boers in Natal needed a commander-in-chief who would say to them "Come," but Joubert only said "Go."

The death of General Joubert in Pretoria, on March 26th, was sincerely re-gretted by all South Africans, for he undoubtedly was one of the most distinguished men in the country. During his long public career he made many friends who held him in high honour for his sterling qualities, his integrity, and his devotion to his country's cause. He made mistakes--and there are few men who are invulnerable to them--but he died while striving to do that which he regarded the best for his country and its cause. If dying for one's country is patriotism, then Joubert's death was sweet.

When war-clouds were gathering and the storm was about to burst over the Transvaal Piet Cronje sat on the stoep of his farmhouse in Potchefstroom, evolving in his mind a system of tactics which he would follow when the conflict began. He was certain that he would be chosen to lead his people, for he had led them in numerous native wars, in the conflict in 1881, and later when Jameson made his ill-starred entry into the Transvaal. Cronje was a man who loved to be amid the quietude of his farm, but he was in the cities often enough to realise that war was the only probable solution of the differences between the Uitlanders and the Boers, and he made preparations for the conflict. He studied foreign military methods and their application to the Boer warfare; he evolved new ideas and improved old ones; he planned battles and the evolutions necessary to win them; he had a natural taste for things military.

Before all the world had heard the blast of the war-trumpet, Cronje had deserted the peaceful stoep and was attacking the enemy on the veld at Mafeking. A victory there, and he was riding at the head of his men toward Kimberley. A skirmish here, a hard-fought battle there, and he had the Diamond City in a state of siege. Victories urged him on, and he led the way southward. A Magersfontein to his wreath, a Belmont and a Graspan--and it seemed as if he were more than nominally the South African Napoleon. A reverse, and Cronje was no longer the dashing, energetic leader of the month before. Doggedly and determinedly he retraced his steps, but advanced cautiously now and then to punish the enemy for its over-confidence. Beaten back to Kimberley by the overpowering force of the enemy, he endured defeat after defeat until finally he was compelled to abandon the siege in order to escape the attacks of a second army sent against him. The enemy's web had been spun around him, but he fought bravely for freedom from entanglement. General French was on one side of him, Lord Roberts on another, Lord Kitchener on a third--and against the experience and troops of all these men was pitted the genius of the Potchefstroom farmer. A fight with Roberts's Horse on Thursday, February 15th; a march of ten miles and a victorious rear-guard action with Lord Kitchener on Friday; a repulse of the forces under Lords Roberts and Kitchener on Saturday, and on Sunday morning the discovery that he and his four thousand men in the river-bed at Paardeberg were surrounded by forty thousand troops of the enemy--that was a four days' record which caused the Lion of Potchefstroom merely to show his fangs to his enemy.

When General Cronje entered the river-bed on Saturday he was certain that he could fight his way out on the following day. Scores of his burghers appealed to him to trek eastward that night, and Commandant-General Ferreira, of the Free State, asked him to trek north-east in order that their two Boer forces might effect a junction, but Cronje was determined to remain in the positions he then occupied until he could carry all his transport-wagons safely away. In the evening Commandants De Beer and Grobler urged the general to escape and explained to him that he would certainly be surrounded the following day, but Cronje steadfastly declined, and expressed his ability to fight a way through any force of the enemy. Even late that night, while the British troops were welding the chain which was to bind him hard and fast in the river-bed, many of Cronje's men begged the general to desert the position, and when they saw him so determined they deserted him and escaped to the eastward.

Cronje might have accepted the advice of his officers and men if he had not believed that he could readily make his way to the east, where he did not suspect the presence of any of Lord Roberts's troops. Not until the following forenoon, when he saw the British advance-guard marching over the hills on the south side of the river, did he realise that the enemy had surrounded him and that he had erred when he determined to hold the position. The grave mistake could not be rectified, and Cronje was in no mood for penitence. He told his men that he expected reinforcements from the east and counselled them to remain cool and fire with discretion until assistance came to them. Later in the day the enemy attacked the camp from all sides but the little army repulsed the onslaught and killed and wounded more than a thousand British soldiers. When the Sabbath sun descended and the four thousand Boers sang their psalms and hymns of thanksgiving there was probably only one man who believed that the burghers would ever be able to escape from the forces which surrounded them, and that man was General Cronje. He realised the gravity of the situation, but he was as calm as if he had been victorious in a battle. He talked cheerily with his men, saying, "Let the English come on," and when they heard their old commander speak in such a confident manner they determined to fight until he himself announced a victory or a defeat.

On Monday morning it seemed as if the very blades of grass for miles around the Boer laager were belching shot and shell over the dongas and trenches where the burghers had sought shelter. Lyddite shells and shrapnel burst over and around them; the bullets of rifles and machine-guns swept close to their heads, and a few yards distant from them were the heavy explosions of ammunition-wagons set on fire by the enemy's shells. Burghers, horses and cattle fell under the storm of lead and iron, and the mingled life-blood of man and beast flowed in rivulets to join the waters of the river. The wounded lay groaning in the trenches; the dead unburied outside, and the cannonading was so terrific that no one was able to leave the trenches and dongas sufficiently long to give a drink of water to a wounded companion. There was no medicine in the camp, all the physicians were held in Jacobsdal by the enemy, and the condition of the dead and dying was such that Cronje was compelled to ask for an armistice. The reply from the British commander was "Fight or surrender," and Cronje chose to continue the fight. The bombardment of the laager was resumed with increased vigour, and there was not a second's respite from shells and bullets until after night descended, when the burghers were enabled to emerge from their trenches and holes to exercise their limbs and to secure food.

The Boers' cannon became defective on Tuesday morning, and thereafter they could reply to the continued bombardment with only their rifles. Hope rose in their breasts during the day when a heliograph message was received from Commandant Froneman; "I am here with Generals De Wet and Cronje," the message read; "Have good cheer. I am waiting for reinforcements. Tell the burghers to find courage in Psalm xxvii." The fact that reinforcements were near, even though the enemy was between, imbued the burghers with renewed faith in their ability to defeat the enemy and, when a concerted attack was made against the laager in the afternoon, a gallant resistance followed.

On Wednesday morning the British batteries again poured their shells on the miserable and exhausted Boers. Shortly before midday there was a lull in the storm, and the beleaguered burghers could hear the reports of the battle between the relieving force and the British troops. The sounds of the fight grew fainter and fainter, then subsided altogether. The bombardment of the laager was renewed, and the burghers realised that Froneman had been beaten back by the enemy. The disappointment was so great that one hundred and fifty Boers bade farewell to their general, and laid down their arms to their enemy. The following day was merely the repetition of the routine of former days, with the exception that the condition of the men and the laager was hourly becoming more miserable. The wounded clamouring for relief was in itself a misery to those who were compelled to hear it, but to allow such appeals to go unanswered was heartrending. To have the dead unburied seemed cruel enough, but to have the corpses before one's eyes day after day was torture. To know that the enemy was in ten times greater strength was disheartening, but to realise that there was no relief at hand was enough to dim the brightest courage. Yet Cronje was undaunted.

Friday and Saturday brought nothing but a message from Froneman, again encouraging them to resist until reinforcements could be brought from Bloemfontein. On Saturday evening Jan Theron, of Krugersdorp, succeeded in breaking through the British lines with despatches from General De Wet and Commandants Cronje and Froneman, urging General Cronje to fight a way through the lines whilst they would engage the enemy from their side. Cronje and his officers decided to make an attempt to escape, and on Sunday morning the burghers commenced the construction of a chain-bridge across the Modder to facilitate the crossing of the swollen river. Fortunately for the Boers the British batteries fired only one shot into the camp that day, and the burghers were able to complete the bridge before night by means of the ropes and chains from their ox-wagons. On Monday morning the British guns made a target of the bridge, and shelled it so unremittingly that no one was able to approach it, much less make an attempt to cross the river by means of it. The bombardment seemed to grow in intensity as the day progressed, and when two shells fell into a group of nine burghers, and left nothing but an arm and a leg to be found, the Krijgsraad decided to hoist a white flag on Tuesday morning. General Cronje and Commandant Schutte were the only officers who voted against surrendering. They begged the other officers to reconsider their decision, and to make an attempt to fight a way out, but the confidence of two men was too weak to change the opinions of the others.

In a position covering less than a square mile of territory, hemmed in on all sides by an army almost as great as that which defeated Napoleon at Waterloo, surrounded by a chain of fire from carbines, rapid-fire guns and heavy cannon, the target of thousands of the vaporous lyddite shells, his trenches enfiladed by a continuous shower of lead, his men half dead from lack of food, and stiff from the effect of their narrow quarters in the trenches, General Cronje chose to fight and to risk complete disaster by leading his four thousand men against the forty thousand of the enemy.

The will of the majority prevailed, and on February 27th, the anniversary of Majuba Hill, after ten days of fighting, the white flag was hoisted above the dilapidated laager. The bodies of ninety-seven burghers lay over the scene of the disaster, and two hundred and forty-five wounded men were left behind when General Cronje and his three thousand six hundred and seventy-nine burghers and women limped out of the river-bed and surrendered to Field-Marshal Lord Roberts.

In many respects General Cronje was the Boers' most brilliant leader, but he was responsible for many serious and costly reverses. At Magersfontein he defeated the enemy fairly, and he might have reaped the fruits of his victory if he had followed up the advantage there gained. Instead, he allowed his army to remain inactive for two months while the British established a camp and base at the river. General French's march to Kimberley might readily have been prevented or delayed if Cronje had placed a few thousand of his men on the low range of kopjes commanding French's route, but during the two days which were so fateful to him and his army General Cronje never stirred from his laager. At Magersfontein Cronje allowed thirty-six cannon, deserted by the British, to remain on several kopjes all of one night and until ten o'clock next morning, when they were taken away by the enemy. When he was asked why he did not send his men to secure the guns Cronje replied, "God has been so good to us that I did not have the heart to send my overworked men to fetch them."

Cronje was absolutely fearless, and in all the battles in which he took part he was always in the most exposed positions. He rarely used a rifle, as one of his eyes was affected, but the short, stoop-shouldered, grey-bearded man, with the long riding-whip, was always in the thick of a fight, encouraging his men and pointing out the positions for attack. He was a fatalist when in battle, if not in times of peace, and it is told of him that at Modder River he was warned by one of the burghers to seek a less exposed position. "If God has ordained me to be shot to-day," the grim old warrior replied, "I shall be shot, whether I sit here or in a well." Cronje was one of the strictest leaders in the Boer army, and that feature made him unpopular with the men who constantly applied to him for leaves-of-absence to return to their homes. They fought for him in the trenches at Paardeberg not because they loved him, but because they respected him as an able leader. He did not have the affection of his burghers like Botha, Meyer, De Wet, or De la Rey, but he held his men together by force of his superior military attainments--a sort of overawing authority which they could not disobey.

Personally, Cronje was not an extraordinary character. He was urbane in manner and a pleasant conversationalist. Like the majority of the Boers he was deeply religious, and tried to introduce the precepts of his religion into his daily life. Although he was sixty-five years old when the war began he had the energy and spirit of a much younger man, and the terrors and anxieties of the ten days' siege at Paardeberg left but little marks on the face which has been described as Christlike. His patriotism was unbounded, and he held the independence of his country above everything. "Independence with peace, if possible, but independence at all costs," he was wont to say, and no one fought harder than he, to attain that end.

When the Vryheid commandos rode over the western border of their district and invaded Natal, Louis Botha, the successor of Commandant-General Joubert, was one of the many Volksraad members who went forth to war in the ranks of the common burghers. After the battle of Dundee, in which he distinguished himself by several daring deeds, Botha became Assistant-General to his lifelong friend and neighbour General Lucas Meyer. Several weeks later, when General Meyer fell ill, he gave his command to his compatriot, General Botha, and a short time afterward, when Commandant-General Joubert was incapacitated by illness, Botha was appointed to assume the responsibilities of the commander-in-chief. When Joubert was on his deathbed he requested that Botha should be his successor, and in that manner Louis Botha, burgher, became Louis Botha, Commandant-General, in less than six months.

It was remarkable, this chain of fortuitous circumstances which led to Botha's rapid advancement, but it was not entirely due to extraneous causes, for he was deserving of every step of his promotion. There is a man for every crisis, but rarely in history is found a record of a soldier who rose from the ranks to commander-in-chief of an army in one campaign. It was Meyer's misfortune when he became ill at a grave period of the war, but it was the country's good fortune to have a Botha ready at hand to fight a Colenso and a Spion Kop. When the burgher army along the Tugela was hard pressed by the enemy and both its old-time leaders, Joubert and Meyer, lay ill at the same time, it seemed little less than providential that a Botha should step out of the ranks and lead the men with as much discretion and valour as could have been expected from the experienced generals whose work he undertook to accomplish. It was a modern representation of the ploughman deserting his farm in order to lead in the salvation of Rome.

Thirty-five years before he was called upon to be Commandant-General of the army of his nation Louis Botha was born near the same spot where he was chosen for that office, and on the soil of the empire against whose forces he was pitting his strength and ability. In his youth he was wont to listen to the narratives of the battles in which his father and grandfather fought side by side against the hordes of natives who periodically dyed the waters of the Tugela crimson with the blood of massacred men and women. In early manhood Botha fought against the Zulus and assisted Lucas Meyer in establishing the New Republic, which afterward became his permanent home. Popularity, ability, and honesty brought him into the councils of the nation as a member of the First Volksraad, where he wielded great influence by reason of his conscientious devotion to duty and his deep interest in the welfare of his country. When public affairs did not require his presence in Pretoria, Botha was with his family on his farm in Vryheid, and there he found the only happiness which he considered worth having. The joys of a pastoral existence combined with the devotion and love of his family were the keystone of Botha's happiness, and no man had a finer realisation of his ambitions in that respect than he. Botha was a warrior, no doubt, but primarily he was a man who loved the peacefulness of a farm, the pleasures of a happy home-life, and the laughter of his four children more than the tramp of victorious troops or the roar of cannon.

There are a few men who have a certain magnetic power which attracts and holds the admiration of others. Louis Botha was a man of this class. Strangers who saw him for the first time loved him. There was an indescribable something about him which caused men looking at him for the first time to pledge their friendship for all time. The light in his blue eyes seemed to mesmerise men, to draw them, willing or unwilling, to him. It was not the quality which gained friends for Kruger nor that which made Joubert popular, but rather a mysterious, involuntary influence which he exerted over everybody with whom he came in contact. A man less handsome, of less commanding appearance than Botha might have possessed such a power, and been considered less extraordinary than he, but it was not wholly his personal appearance--for he was the handsomest man in the Boer army--which aroused the admiration of men. His voice, his eyes, his facial expression and his manner--all combined to strengthen the man's power over others. It may have been personal magnetism or a mysterious charm which he possessed--but it was the mark of a great man.

The early part of Botha's career as a general was fraught with many difficulties, the majority of which could be traced to his lack of years. The Boer mind could not grasp the fact that a man of thirty-five years could be a military leader, and for a long time the Boers treated the young commander with a certain amount of contempt. The old takhaars laughed at him when he asked them to perform any duties, and called him a boy. They were unable to understand for a long time why they should act upon the advice or orders of a man many years younger than they themselves, and it was not until Botha had fought Colenso and Spion Kop that the old burghers commenced to realise that ability was not always monopolised by men with hoary beards. Before they had these manifestations of Botha's military genius hundreds of the burghers absolutely refused to obey his commands, and even went to the length of protesting to the Government against his continued tenure of the important post.

The younger Boers, however, were quicker to discern the worth of the man, and almost without exception gave him their united support. There was one instance when a young Boer questioned Botha's authority, but the burgher's mind was quickly disabused, and thereafter he was one of the Commandant-General's staunchest supporters. It was at the battle of Pont Drift, when General Botha was busily engaged in directing the movements of his men and had little time to argue fine points of authority. The general asked two young Boers to carry ammunition to the top of a kopje which was being hard-shelled by the enemy. One of the Boers was willing immediately to obey the general, but the other man refused to undertake the hazardous journey. The general spoke kindly to the Boer, and acknowledged that he would be risking his life by ascending the hill, but insisted that he should go. The Boer finally declared he would not go, and added that Botha was too young to give orders to men. The Commandant-General did not lose his temper, but it did not require much time for him to decide that a rebuke of some sort was necessary, so he knocked the man to the ground with his fist. It was a good, solid blow, and the young Boer did not move for a minute, but when he rose he had fully decided that he would gladly carry the ammunition to the top of the kopje.

After General Botha demonstrated that he was a capable military leader he became the idol of all the Boers. His popularity was second only to that of President Kruger, and the hero-worshippers arranged for all sorts of honours to be accorded to him after the war. He was to be made President, first of all things; then his birthday anniversary was to be made the occasion of a national holiday; statues were to be erected for him, and nothing was to be left undone in order that his services to his country might be given the appreciation they deserved. The stoical Boers were never known to worship a man so idolatrously as they did in this case, and it was all the more noteworthy on account of the adverse criticism which was bestowed upon him several months before.

General Botha's reputation as a gallant and efficient leader was gained during the campaign in Natal, but it was not until after the relief of Ladysmith that his real hard work began. After the advance of Lord Roberts's large army from Bloemfontein was begun myriads of new duties devolved upon the Commandant-General, and thereafter he displayed a skill and ingenuity in dealing with grave situations which was marvellous, when it is taken into consideration that he was opposing a victorious army with a mere handful of disappointed and gloomy burghers. The situation would have been grave enough if he had had a trained and disciplined army under his command, but in addition to making plans for opposing the enemy's advance, General Botha was compelled to gather together the burghers with whom he desired to make the resistance. His work would have been comparatively easy if he could have remained at the spot where his presence was most necessary, but it was absolutely impossible for him to lead the defensive movements in the Free State without men, and in order to secure them he was obliged to desert that important post and go to the Biggarsberg, where many burghers were idle. Telegraph wires stretched from the Free State to Natal, but a command sent by such a route never caused a burgher to move an inch nearer to the Free State front, and consequently the Commandant-General was compelled to go personally to the Biggarsberg in search of volunteers to assist the burghers south of Kroonstad. When General Botha arrived in Natal in the first days of May he asked the Standerton commando to return with him to the Free State. They flatly refused to go unless they were first allowed to spend a week at their homes, but Botha finally, after much begging, cajoling, and threatening, induced the burghers to go immediately. The Commandant-General saw the men board a train, and then sped joyously northward toward Pretoria and the Free State in a special train. When he reached Pretoria Botha learned that the Standerton commando followed him as far as Standerton station, and then dispersed to their homes. His dismay was great; but he was not discouraged, and several hours later he was at Standerton, riding from farm to farm to gather the men. This work delayed his arrival in the Free State two days, but he secured the entire commando, and went with it to the front, where it served him valiantly.

The masterly retreat of the Boer forces northward along the railway and across the Vaal River, and the many skirmishes and battles with which Botha harassed the enemy's advance, were mere incidents in the Commandant-General's work of those trying days. There were innumerable instances not unlike that in connection with the Standerton commando, and, in addition, there was the planning to prevent the large commandos in the western part of the Transvaal, and Meyer's large force in the south-eastern part, from being cut off from his own body of burghers. It was a period of grave moment and responsibilities, but Botha was the man for the occasion. Although the British succeeded in entering Pretoria, the capital of the country, the Boers lost little in prestige or men, and Botha and his burghers were as confident of the final success of their cause as they were when they crossed the Natal border seven months before. Even after all the successive defeats of his army, Commandant-General Botha continued to say, "We will fight--fight until not a single British soldier remains on South African soil." A general who can express such a firm faith in his cause when he sees nothing but disaster surrounding him is great even if he is not always victorious.

The military godfather of Commandant-General Botha was General Lucas Meyer, one of the best leaders in the Boer army. The work of the two men was cast in almost the same lines during the greater part of the campaign, and many of the Commandant-General's burdens were shared by his old-time tutor and neighbour in the Vryheid district. Botha seldom undertook a project unless he first consulted with Meyer, and the two constantly worked hand-in-hand. Their friends frequently referred to them as Damon and Pythias, and the parallel was most appropriate, for they were as nearly the counterparts of those old Grecian warriors as modern limitations would allow. Botha attained the post of Commandant-General through the illness of Meyer, who would undoubtedly have been Joubert's successor if he had not fallen ill at an important period of the campaign, but the fact that the pupil became the superior officer of the instructor never strained the amicable relations of the two men.

General Meyer received his fundamental military education from the famous Zulu chieftain, Dinizulu, in 1884, when he and eight hundred other Boers assisted the natives in a war against the chieftains of other tribes. In a battle at Labombo mountain, June 6th of that year, Meyer and Dinizulu vanquished the enemy, and as payment for their services the Boers each received a large farm in the district now known as Vryheid. A Government named the New Republic was organised by the farmers, and Meyer was elected President, a post which he held for four years, when the Transvaal annexed the republic to its own territory. In the war of 1881 Meyer took part in several battles, and at Ingogo he was struck on the head by a piece of shell, which caused him to be unconscious for forty-two days. In the later days of the republic General Meyer held various military and civil positions in the Vryheid district, where his large farm, "Anhouwen," is located, and was the chairman of the Volksraad which decided to send the ultimatum to Great Britain.

When war was actually declared, General Meyer, with his commandos, was on the Transvaal border near his farm, and he opened hostilities by making a bold dash into Natal and attacking the British army encamped at Dundee. The battle was carefully planned by Meyer, and it would undoubtedly have ended with the capture of the entire British force if General Erasmus, who was to co-operate with him, had fulfilled the part assigned to him. Although many British soldiers were killed and captured, and great stores of ammunition and equipment taken, the forces under General Yule were allowed to escape to the south. General Meyer followed the fleeing enemy as rapidly as the muddy roads could be traversed, and engaged them at Modderspruit. There he gained a decisive victory, and compelled the survivors to enter Ladysmith, where they were immediately besieged. Meyer was extremely ill before the battle began, but he insisted upon directing his men, and continued to do so until the field was won, when he fell from his horse, and was seriously ill for a month. He returned to the front, against the advice of his physicians, on December 24th, and took part in the fighting at Pont Drift, Boschrand, and in the thirteen days' battle around Pieter's Hill. In the battle of Pont Drift a bullet struck the General's field-glasses, flattened itself, and dropped into one of his coat pockets, to make a souvenir brooch for Mrs. Meyer, who frequently visited him when no important movements were in progress.

When General Joubert and his Krijgsraad determined to retreat from the Tugela and allow Ladysmith to be relieved, General Meyer was one of those who protested against such a course, and when the decision was made Meyer returned to the Tugela, and remained there with his friend Louis Botha during the long and heroic fight against General Buller's column. Meyer and Botha were among the last persons to leave the positions which they had defended so long, and on their journey northward the two generals decided to return and renew the fight as soon as they could reach Modderspruit and secure food for their men and horses. When they arrived at Modderspruit they found that Joubert and his entire army had fled northward, and had carried with them every ounce of food. It was a bitter disappointment to the two generals, but there was nothing to be done except to travel in the direction of the scent of food, and the journey led the dejected, disappointed, starved generals and burghers north over the Biggarsberg mountains, where provisions could be secured.

During the long period in March and April when neither Boers nor British seemed to be doing anything, General Meyer arranged a magnificent series of entrenchments in the Biggarsberg mountains which made an advance of the enemy practically impossible. Foreign military experts pronounced the defence impregnable and expressed the greatest astonishment when they learned that Meyer formulated the plans of the entrenchments without ever having read a book on the subject or without having had the benefit of any instruction. The entrenchments began at a point a few miles east of the British outposts and continued for miles and miles north-east and north-west to the very apex of the Biggarsberg. Spruits and rivers were connected by means of trenches so that a large Boer force could travel many miles without being observed by the enemy, and the series of entrenchments was fashioned in such a manner that the Boers could retreat to the highest point of the mountains and remain meanwhile in perfect concealment. Near the top of the mountain long schanzes or walls were built to offer a place of security for the burghers, while on the top were miles of walls to attract and to inveigle the enemy to approach the lower wall more closely. The plan was magnificent, but the British forces evaded the Biggarsberg in their advance movements, and the entrenchments were never bathed in human blood.

When the Boers in the Free State were unable to stem the advance of the British, General Meyer was compelled to retreat northward to ensure his own safety, but he did it so slowly and systematically that he lost only a few men and was able, now and then, to make bold dashes at the enemy's flying columns with remarkable success. The retreat northward through the Transvaal was fraught with many harassments, but General Meyer joined forces with General Botha east of Pretoria and thereafter the teacher and pupil again fought hand in hand in a common cause.

COMMANDANT-GENERAL CHRISTIAN H. DE WET

The Free State was not as prolific of generals as the Transvaal, but in Christian De Wet she had one of the ablest as well as one of the most fearless leaders in the Republican ranks. Before he was enlisted to fight for his country De Wet was a farmer, who had a penchant for dealing in potatoes, and his only military training was secured when he was one of the sixty Boer volunteers who ascended the slopes of Majuba Hill in 1881. There was nothing of the military in his appearance; in fact, Christian De Wet, Commandant-General of the Orange Free State in 1900, was not a whit unlike Christian De Wet, butcher of Barberton of 1879, and men who knew him in the gold-rush days of that mining town declared that he was more martial in appearance then as a licensed slayer of oxen than later as a licensed slayer of men. He himself prided himself on his unmilitary exterior, and it was not a little source of satisfaction to him to say that his fighting regalia was the same suit of clothing which he wore on his farm on the day that he left it to fight as a soldier in his country's army.

Before the war, De Wet's chief claim to notoriety lay in the fact that he attempted to purchase the entire supply of potatoes in South Africa for the purpose of effecting a "corner" of that product on the Johannesburg market. Unfortunately for himself, he held his potatoes until the new crop was harvested, and he became a bankrupt in consequence. Later he appeared as a potato farmer near Kroonstad, and still later, at Nicholson's Nek in Natal, he captured twelve hundred British prisoners and, incidentally, a large stock of British potatoes, which seemed to please him almost as greatly as the human captives. Although the vegetable strain was frequently predominant in De Wet's constitution, he was not over-zealous to return to his former pastoral pursuits, and continued to lead his commandos over the hills of the eastern Free State long after that territory was christened the Orange River Colony.

General De Wet was at the head of a number of the Free State commandos which crossed into Natal at the outbreak of the war, and he took part in several of the battles around Ladysmith; but his services were soon required in the vicinity of Kimberley, and there he made an heroic effort to effect a junction with the besieged Cronje. It was not until after the British occupation of Bloemfontein that De Wet really began his brilliant career as a daring commander, but thereafter he was continually harassing the enemy. He led with three big battles in one week, with a total result of a thousand prisoners of war, seven cannon, and almost half a million pounds' worth of supplies. At Sannaspost, on March 31st, he swept down upon Colonel Broadwood's column and captured one-fourth of the men and all their vast supplies almost before the British officer was aware of the presence of the enemy. The echoes of that battle had hardly subsided when he fell upon another British column at Moester's Hoek with results almost as great as at Sannaspost, and two days later he was besieging a third British column in his own native heath of Wepener. Column after column was sent to drive him away, but he clung fast to his prey for almost two weeks, when he eluded the great force on his capture bent, and moved northward to take an active part in opposing the advance of Lord Roberts. He led his small force of burghers as far as the northern border of the Free State, while the enemy advanced, and then turned eastward, carrying President Steyn and the capital of the Republic with him to places of safety. Whenever there was an opportunity he sent small detachments to attack the British lines of communications and harassed the enemy continually. In almost all his operations the Commandant-General was assisted by his brother, General Peter De Wet, who was none the less daring in his operations. Christian De Wet was responsible for more British losses than any of the other generals. In his operations in Natal and the Free State he captured more than three thousand prisoners, thousands of cattle and horses, and stores and ammunition valued at more than a million pounds. The number of British soldiers killed and wounded in battles with De Wet is a matter for conjecture, but it is not limited by the one thousand mark.

GENERAL PETER DE WET

General John De la Rey, who operated in the Free State with considerable success, was one of the most enthusiastic leaders in the army, and his confidence in the Boers' fighting ability was not less than his faith in the eventual success of their arms. De la Rey was born on British soil, but he had a supreme contempt for the British soldier, and frequently asserted that one burgher was able to defeat ten soldiers at any time or place. He was the only one of the generals who was unable to speak the English language, but he understood it well enough to capture a spy whom he overheard in a Free State hotel. De la Rey was a Transvaal general, and when the retreat from Bloemfontein was made he harassed the enemy greatly, but was finally compelled to cross the Vaal into his own country, where he continued to fight under Commandant-General Botha.

Among the other Boer generals who took active part in the campaign in other parts of the Republics were J. Du P. De Beer, a Raad member, who defended the northern border of the Transvaal; Sarel Du Toit, whose defence at Fourteen Streams was admirably conducted; Snyman, the old Marico farmer, who besieged Mafeking; Hendrik Schoeman, who operated in Cape Colony; Jan Kock, killed at the Elandslaagte battle early in the campaign; and the three generals, Lemmer, Grobler, and Olivier, whose greatest success was their retreat from Cape Colony.

GENERAL JOHN DE LA REY

The Boer generals and officers, almost without exception, were admirable men, personally. Some of them were rough, hardy men, who would have felt ill at ease in a drawing-room, but they had much of the milk of human kindness in them, and there was none who loved to see or partake of bloodshed. There may have been instances when white or Red Cross flags were fired upon, but when such a breach of the rules of war occurred it was not intentional. The foreigners who accompanied the various Boer armies--the correspondents, military attachés, and the volunteers--will testify that the officers, from Commandant-General Botha down to the corporals, were always zealous in their endeavours to conduct an honourable warfare, and that the farmer-generals were as gentlemanly as they were valorous.

8. The War Presidents

The real leader of the Boers of the two Republics was Paul Kruger, their man of peace. His opinions on the momentous questions that agitated the country and his long political supremacy caused him many and bitter enemies, but the war healed all animosities and he was the one man in the Republics who had the respect, love, and admiration of all the burghers. Wherever one might be, whether in the houses on the veld or in the battlefield's trenches, every one spoke of "Oom Paul" in a manner which indicated that he was the Boer of all Boers. There was not one burgher who would not declare that Kruger was a greater man than he was before he despatched his famous ultimatum to Great Britain. His old-time friends supported him even more faithfully than before hostilities began, and his political energies of other days became the might of his right arm. Those who opposed him most bitterly and unremittingly when it was a campaign between the Progressive and Conservative parties were most eager to listen to his counsels and to stand by his side when their country's hour of darkness had arrived. Not a word of censure for him was heard anywhere; on the contrary, every one praised him for opposing Great Britain so firmly, and prayed that his life might be spared until their dream of absolute independence was realised.

Sir Charles Dilke once related a conversation he had with Bismarck concerning Paul Kruger. "Cavour was much smarter, more clever, more diplomatically gifted than I," said the Prince, "but there is a much stronger, much abler man than Cavour or I, and that man is President Kruger. He has no gigantic army behind him, no great empire to support him. He stands alone with a small peasant people, and is a match for us by mere force of genius. I spoke to him--he drove me into a corner." Kruger's great ability, as delineated by Bismarck, was indisputable, and a man with less of it might have been President and might have avoided the war, but only at a loss to national interests. The President had one aim and one goal, his country's independence, and all the force of his genius was directed toward the attainment of that end. He tried to secure his country's total independence by peaceable means, but he had planted the seed of that desire so deeply in the minds of his countrymen that when it sprouted they overwhelmed him and he was driven into war against his will. Kruger would not have displaced diplomacy with the sword, but his burghers felt that peaceful methods of securing their independence were of no avail, and he was powerless to resist their wishes. He did not lead the Boers into war; they insisted that only war would give to them the relief they desired, and he followed under their leadership. When the meetings of the Volksraad immediately preceding the war were held, it was not Paul Kruger who called for war; it was the representatives of the burghers, who had been instructed by their constituents to act in such a manner. When the President saw that his people had determined to have war, he was leader enough to make plans which might bring the conflict to a successful conclusion, and he chose a moment for making a declaration that he considered opportune. The ultimatum was decided upon eleven days before it was actually despatched, but it was delayed eight days on account of the Free State's unpreparedness. Kruger realised the importance of striking the first blow at an enemy which was not prepared to resist it, and the Free State's tardiness at such a grave crisis was decidedly unpleasant to him. Then, when the Free State was ready to mobilise, the President secured another delay of three days in order that diplomacy might have one more chance. His genius had not enabled him to realise the dream of his life without a recourse to war, and when the ultimatum was delivered into the hands of the British the old man wept.

When the multitudinous executive duties to which he attended in peaceful times were suddenly ended by the declaration, the President busied himself with matters pertaining to the conduct of the war. He worked as hard as any man in the country, despite his age, and on many occasions he displayed the energy of a man many years younger. The war caused his daily routine of work and rest to be changed completely. He continued to rise at four o'clock in the morning, a habit which he contracted in early youth and followed ever after. After his morning devotions he listened to the reading of the despatches from the generals at the front, and dictated replies in the shape of suggestions, censure, or praise. He slept for an hour after breakfast, and then went to the Government Buildings, arriving there punctually every morning as the clock on the dome struck nine. He remained in consultation with the other members of the Executive Council and the few Government officials, who had remained in the city, for an hour or more. After luncheon he again worked over despatches, received burghers on leave of absence from the front and foreigners who sympathised with his people's cause. He never allowed himself to be idle, and, in fact, there was no opportunity for him to be unemployed, inasmuch as almost all the leading Government officials were at the front, while many of their duties remained behind to be attended to by some one. Kruger himself supervised the work of all the departments whose heads were absent, and the labour was great. His capacity for hard labour was never better demonstrated than during the war, when he bore the weight of his own duties and those of other Government officials, as well as the work of guiding the Boer emissaries in foreign countries. Added to all these grave responsibilities, when the reverses of the army grew more serious, was the great worry and the constant dread of new disasters which beset a man who occupies a position such as he occupied.

PRESIDENT KRUGER ADDRESSING AMERICAN VOLUNTEERS

No man had greater influence over the Boers than Kruger, and his counsel was always sought and his advice generally followed. When the first commandos went to the front it was considered almost absolutely necessary for them to stop at Pretoria and see "Oom Paul" before going to battle, and it seemed to affect the old man strangely when he addressed them and bade them God-speed in the accomplishment of their task. It was in the midst of one of these addresses that the President, while standing in the centre of a group of burghers, broke down and wept as he referred to the many men who would lose their lives in the war. When the Boer army was having its greatest successes Kruger constantly sent messages to his burghers, thanking them for their good work, and reminding them not to neglect thanking their God for His favours. One of the most characteristic messages of this nature was sent to the generals, commandants, officers, and burghers on January 8th, and was a most unique ebullition to come from a President of a Republic. The message was composed by himself, and, as literally translated, read:--

"For your own and the war-officers' information, I wish to state that, through the blessing of our Lord, our great cause has at present been carried to such a point that, by dint of great energy, we may expect to bring it to a successful issue on our behalf.

"In order that such an end be attained, it is, however, strictly necessary that all energy be used, that all burghers able to do active service go forward to the battlefield, and that those who are on furlough claim no undue extension thereof, but return as soon as possible, every one to the place where his war-officers may be stationed.

"Brothers! I pray you to act herein with all possible promptitude and zeal, and to keep your eyes fixed on that Providence who has miraculously led our people through the whole of South Africa. Read Psalm 33, from verse 7 to the end.

"The enemy have fixed their faith in Psalm 83, where it is said that this people shall not exist and its name must be annihilated; but the Lord says: 'It shall exist' Read also Psalm 89, the 13th and 14th verses, where the Lord saith that the children of Christ, if they depart from His words, shall be chastised with bitter reverses, but His favour and goodness shall have no end and never fail. What He has said remains strong and firm. For, see, the Lord purifieth His children, even unto gold, proven by fire.

"I need not draw your attention to all the destructiveness of the enemy's works, for you know it, and I again point to the attack of the Devil on Christ and His Church. This has been the attack from the beginning, and God will not countenance the destruction of His Church. You know that our cause is a just one, and there cannot be any doubt, for it is with the contents of just this Psalm that they commenced with us in their wickedness, and I am still searching the entire Bible, and find no other way which can be followed than that which has been followed by us, and we must continue to fight in the name of the Lord.

"Please notify all the officers of war and the entire public of your district of the contents of this telegram, and imbue them with a full earnestness of the cause."

When the President learned that Commandant-General Joubert had determined to retreat from the neighbourhood of Ladysmith he sent a long telegram to his old friend, imploring him not to take such a step, and entreating him to retain his forces at the Tugela. The old General led his forces northward to Glencoe, notwithstanding the President's protest, and a day afterward Kruger arrived on the scene. The President was warrior enough to know that a great mistake had been made, and he did not hesitate to show his displeasure. He and Joubert had had many disagreements in their long experiences with one another, but those who were present in the General's tent at that Glencoe interview said that they had never seen the President so angry. When he had finished giving his opinion of the General's action the President shook Joubert's hand, and thereafter they discussed matters calmly and as if there had been no quarrel. To the other men who were partly responsible for the retreat he showed his resentment of their actions by declining to shake hands with them, a method of showing disapprobation that is most cutting to the Boers.

"If I were five years younger, or if my eyesight were better," he growled at the recalcitrants, "I would take a rifle and bandolier and show you what we old Boers were accustomed to do. We had courage; you seem to have none."

After the President had encouraged the officers, and had secured their promises to continue the resistance against their enemy he wandered about in the laagers, shaking hands with and infusing new spirit into the burghers who had flocked together to see their revered leader. When several thousand of the Boers had gathered around him and were trying to have a word with him the President bared his head and asked his friends to join him in prayer. Instantly every head was bared, and Kruger's voice spread out over the vast concourse in a grand appeal to the God of Battles to grant His blessing to the burgher army. The grey-haired old man was conspicuous in a small circle which was formed by the burghers withdrawing several paces when he began the prayer. On all sides there spread out a mass of black-garbed, battle-begrimed Boers with eyes turned to the ground. Here and there a white tent raised its head above the assemblage; at other points men stood on wagons and cannon. Farther on, burghers dismounted from their horses and joined the crowd. In the distance were Talana Hill, where the first battle of the campaign was fought; the lofty Drakensberg where more than fifty years before the early Boer Voortrekkers had their first glimpses of fair

Natal, while to the south were the hills of Ladysmith of sombre history. There in the midst of bloody battlefields, and among several thousand men who sought the blood of the enemy, Kruger, the man of peace, implored Almighty God to give strength to his burghers. It was a magnificent spectacle.

He had been at Glencoe only a short time when the news reached him that the burghers in the Free State had lost their courage, and were retreating rapidly towards Bloemfontein. He abbreviated his visit, hastened to the Free State, and met the fleeing Boers at Poplar Grove. He exhorted them to make a stand against the enemy, and, by his magnetic power over them, succeeded in inducing the majority to remain and oppose the British advance. His own fearlessness encouraged them, and when they saw their old leader standing in the midst of shell fire as immobile as if he were watching a holiday parade, they had not the heart to run. While he was watching the battle a shell fell within a short distance of where he stood, and all his companions fled from the spot. He walked slowly away, and when the men returned to him he chided them, and made a witty remark concerning the shell, naming it one of "the Queen's pills." While the battle continued, Kruger followed one of the commandos and urged the men to fight. At one stage of the battle the commando which he was following was in imminent danger of being cut off and captured by the British forces, but the burghers fought valiantly before their President, and finally conveyed him to a place of safety, although the path was shell and bullet swept.

He returned to Bloemfontein, and in conjunction with President Steyn, addressed an appeal to Lord Salisbury to end the war. They asked that the republics should be allowed to retain their independence, and firmly believed that the appeal would end hostilities, inasmuch as the honours of war were then about equally divided between the two armies. To those who watched the proceedings it seemed ridiculous to ask for a cessation of hostilities at that time, but Kruger sincerely believed that his appeal would not be in vain, and he was greatly surprised, but not discomfited, when a distinct refusal was received in reply.

Several weeks after the memorable trip to the Free State, President Kruger made another journey to the sister-republic, and met President Steyn and all the Boer generals at the famous Krijgsraad at Kroonstad. No one who heard the President when he addressed the burghers who gathered there to see him, will ever forget the intensity of Kruger's patriotism. Kroonstad, then the temporary capital of the Free State, was not favoured with any large public hall where a meeting might be held, so a small butcher's stand in the market-square was chosen for the site of the meeting. After President Steyn, Commandant-General Joubert, and several other leading Boers had addressed the large crowd of burghers standing in the rain outside the tradesman's pavilion, Kruger stepped on one of the long tables, and exhorted the burghers to renewed efforts, to fight for freedom and not to be disconsolate because Bloemfontein had fallen into the hands of the enemy. When the President concluded his address the burghers raised a great cheer, and then returned to their laagers with their minds filled with a new spirit, and with renewed determination to oppose the enemy--a determination which displayed itself later in the fighting at Sannaspost, Moester's Hoek, and Wepener. Kruger found the burghers in the Free State in the depths of despair; when he departed they were as confident of ultimate victory as they were on the day war was begun. The old man had the faculty of leading men as it is rarely found. In times of peace he led men by force of argument as much as by reason of personal magnetism. In war-time he led men by mere words sent over telegraph wires, by his presence at the front, and by his display of manly dignity, firm resolution and devotion to his country. He was like the kings and rulers of ancient times, who led their cohorts into battle, and wielded the sword when there was a necessity for such action.

During the war President Kruger suffered many disappointments, endured many griefs, and withstood many trials and tribulations; but none affected him so deeply as the death of his intimate friend, Commandant-General Joubert. Kruger and Joubert were the two leading men of the country for many years. They were among those who assisted in the settlement of the Transvaal and in the many wars which were coincident with it. They had indelibly inscribed their names on the scroll of the South African history of a half-century, and in doing so they had become as intimate as two brothers. For more than two score years Kruger had been considered the Boers' leader in peaceful times, while Joubert was the Boers' warrior. The ambition of both was the independence of their country, and, while they differed radically on the methods by which it was to be attained, neither surpassed the other in strenuous efforts to secure it without a recourse to war. The death of Joubert was as saddening to Kruger, consequently, as the Demise of his most dearly-beloved brother could have been, and in the funeral-oration which the President delivered over the bier of the General, he expressed that sense of sorrow most aptly. This oration, delivered upon an occasion when the country was mourning the death of a revered leader and struggling under the weight of recent defeats, was one of the most remarkable utterances ever made by a man at the head of a nation.

"Brothers, sisters, burghers, and friends," he began,--"Only a few words can I say to you to-day, for the spirit is willing, but the flesh is weak. We have lost our brother, our friend, our Commandant-General. I have lost my right hand, not of yesterday, but my right hand since we were boys together, many long years ago. To-night I alone seem to have been spared of the old people of our cherished land, of the men who lived and struggled together for our country. He has gone to heaven whilst fighting for liberty, which God has told us to defend; for the freedom for which he and I have struggled together for so many years, and so often, to maintain. Brothers, what shall I say to you in this our greatest day of sorrow, in this hour of national gloom? The struggle we are engaged in is for the principles of justice and righteousness, which our Lord Has taught us is the broad road to heaven and blessedness. It is our sacred duty to keep on that path, if we desire a happy ending. Our dear dead brother has gone on that road to his eternal life. What can I say of his personality? It is only a few short weeks ago that I saw him at the fighting front, humbly and modestly taking his share of the privations and the rough work of the campaign like the poorest burgher, a true general, a true Christian--an example to his people. And he spoke to me then and even more recently; and, let me tell you, that the days are dark. We are suffering reverses on account of wickedness rampant in our land. No success will come, no blessings be given to our great cause unless you remove the bad elements from among us; and then you may look forward to attaining the crowning point, the reward of righteousness and noble demeanour. We have in our distinguished departed brother an example. Chosen, as he was, by the nation, time after time, to his honourable position, he had their trust to such an extent that everything was left in his hands; and he did his work well. He died, as he has lived, in the path of duty and honour. Let the world rage around us, let the enemy decry us, I say, Follow his example. The Lord will stand by you against the ruthless hand of the foe, and at the moment when He deems it right for interference peace will come once more. Why is the sympathy of the whole world with us in this struggle for freedom? Why are the strangers pouring in from Europe to assist to the maintenance of our beloved flag, to aid us in the just defence of our independence? Is it not God's hand? I feel it in my heart. I declare to you again, the end of our struggle will be satisfactory. Our small nation exists by the aid of the Almighty, and will continue to do so. The prophets say the closed books shall be opened, the dead shall arise, darkness be turned into light; nothing be concealed. Every one will face God's judgment throne. You will listen to His voice, and your eyes shall be open for the truth of everything. Think of the costly lives given by us for our cause, and you will rally to the fight for justice to the end. Brothers, to the deeply bereaved widow of our Commandant-General, to his family, to you all, I say trust more than ever in the Almighty; go to Him for condolence; think and be trustful in the thought that our brother's body has gone from amongst us to rise again in a beautiful and eternal home. Let us follow his example. Weep not, the Lord will support you; the hour of all our relief is near; and let us pray that we may enter heaven, and be guided to eternity in the same way as he whom we mourn so deeply. Amen."

Early in his life Kruger formed an idea that the Boers were under the direct control of Providence, and it displeased him greatly to learn that many petty thefts were committed by some of the burghers at the front. In many of the speeches to the burghers he referred to the shortcomings of some of them, and tried to impress on their minds, that they could never expect the Lord to took with favour on their cause if they did not mend their ways. He made a strong reference to those sins in the oration he delivered over Joubert's body, and never neglected to tell the foreign volunteers that they had come into the country for fighting and not for looting. When an American corps of about fifty volunteers arrived in Pretoria in April he requested that they should call at his residence before leaving for the front, and the men were greatly pleased to receive and accept the invitation. The President walked to the sidewalk in front of his house to receive the Americans, and then addressed them in this characteristically blunt speech: "I am very glad you have come here to assist us. I want you to look after your horses and rifles. Do not allow any one to steal them from you. Do not steal anybody else's gun or horse. Trust in God, and fight as hard as you can."

Undoubtedly one of the most pathetic incidents in Kruger's life was his departure from Pretoria when the British army was only a short distance south of that city. It was bitter enough to him to witness the conquest of the veld district, the farms and the plantations, but when the conquerors were about to possess the capital of the country which he himself had seen growing out of the barren veld into a beautiful city of brick and stone, it was indeed a grave epoch for an old man to pass through. It hurt him little to see Johannesburg fall to the enemy, for that city was ever in his enemy's hands, but when Pretoria, distinctly the Boer city, was about to become British, perhaps for ever, the old man might have been expected to display signs of the great sorrow which he undoubtedly felt in his heart. At the threshold of such a great calamity to his cause it might have been anticipated that he would acknowledge defeat and ask for mercy from a magnanimous foe. It was not dreamt of that a man of almost four score years would desert his home and family, his farms and flocks, the result of a lifetime's labour, and endure the discomforts of the field merely because he believed in a cause which, it seemed, was about to be extinguished by force of arms. But adversity caused no changes in the President's demeanour. When he bade farewell to his good old wife--perhaps it was a final farewell--he cheered and comforted her, and when the weeping citizens and friends of many years gathered at his little cottage to bid him goodbye he chided them for their lack of faith in the cause, and encouraged them to believe that victory would crown the Boers' efforts.

Seven months before, Kruger stood on the verandah of his residence, and, doffing his hat to the first British prisoners that arrived in the city, asked his burghers not to rejoice unseemingly; in May the old man, about to flee before the enemy, inspired his people to take new courage, and ridiculed their ideas that all was lost.

Whether the Boers were in the first flush of victory or in the depths of despair Paul Kruger was ever the same to them--patriot, adviser, encourager, leader, and friend.

It was an easy matter to see the President when he was at his residence at Pretoria, and he appeared to be deeply interested in learning the opinions of the many foreigners who arrived in his country. The little verandah of the Executive Mansion--a pompous name for the small, one-storey cottage--was the President's favourite resting and working place during the day. Just as in the days of peace he sat there in a big armchair, discussing politics with groups of his countrymen, so while the war was in progress he was seated there pondering the grave subjects of the time. The countrymen who could always be observed with him at almost any time of the day were missing. They were at the front. Occasionally two or three old Boers could be seen chatting with him behind Barnato's marble lions, but invariably they had bandoliers around their bodies and rifles across their knees. Few of the old Boers who knew the President intimately returned from the front on leaves-of-absence unless they called on him to explain to him the tide and progress of the war.

According to his own declaration his health was as good as it ever was, although the war added many burdens to his life. Although he was seventy-five years old he declared he was as sprightly as he was twenty years before, and he seemed to have the energy and vitality of a man of forty. The reports that his mind was affected were cruel hoaxes which had not the slightest foundation of fact. The only matter concerning which he worried was his eyesight, which had been growing weaker steadily for five years. That misfortune alone prevented him from accompanying his burghers to the front and sharing their burdens with them, and he frequently expressed his disappointment that he was unable to engage more actively in the defence of his country. When Pretoria fell into British hands Kruger again sacrificed his own interests for the welfare of his Government and moved the capital into the fever-districts, the low-veld of the eastern part of the Transvaal. The deadly fever which permeates the atmosphere of that territory seemed to have no more terrors for him than did the British bullets at Poplar Grove, and he chose to remain in that dangerous locality in order that he might be in constant communication with his burghers and the outside world rather than to go farther into the isolated interior where he would have assumed no such great risks to his health.

Mr. Kruger was not a bitter enemy of the British nation, as might have been supposed. He was always an admirer of Britons and British institutions, and the war did not cause him to alter his convictions. He despised only the men whom he charged with being responsible for the war, and he never thought to hide the identity of those men. He blamed Mr. Rhodes, primarily, for instigating the war, and held Mr. Chamberlain and Sir Alfred Milner equally responsible for bringing it about. Against these three men he was extremely bitter, and he took advantage of every opportunity for expressing his opinions of them and their work. In February he stated that the real reason of the war between the Boers and the British was Rhodes's desire for glory. "He wants to be known as the maker of the South African empire," he said, "and the empire is not complete so long as there are two Republics in the centre of the country."

Whatever were the causes of the war, it is certain that President Kruger did not make it in order to gain political supremacy in the country. The Dutch of Cape Colony, President Steyn of the Free State, and Secretary Reitz of the Transvaal, may have had visions of Dutch supremacy, but President Kruger had no such hopes. He invariably and strenuously denied that he had any aspirations other than the independence of his country, and all his words and works emphasised his statement to that effect. Several days before Commandant-General Joubert died, that intimate friend of the President declared solemnly that Kruger had never dreamt of expelling the British Government from South Africa and much less had made any agreement with the Dutch in other parts of the country with a view to such a result. It was a difficult matter to find a Transvaal Boer or a Boer from the northern part of the Free State who cared whether the British or the Dutch were paramount in South Africa so long as the Republics were left unharmed, but it was less difficult to meet Cape Colonists and Boers from the southern part of the Free State who desired that Great Britain's power in the country should be broken. If there was any real spirit against Great Britain it was born on British soil in Cape Colony and blown northward to where courage to fight was more abundant. Its source certainly was not in the north, and more certainly not with Paul Kruger, the man of peace.

President Steyn, of the Orange Free State, occupied even a more responsible position than his friend President Kruger, of the Transvaal. At the beginning of hostilities, Steyn found that hundreds of the British-born citizens of his State refused to fight with his army, and consequently he was obliged to join the Transvaal with a much smaller force than he had reckoned upon. He was handicapped by the lack of generals of any experience, and he did not have a sufficient number of burghers to guard the borders of his own State. His Government had made but few preparations for war, and there was a lack of guns, ammunition, and equipment. The mobilisation of his burghers was extremely difficult and required much more time than was anticipated, and everything seemed to be awry at a time when every detail should have been carefully planned and executed. As the responsible head of the Government and the veritable head of the army Steyn passed a crisis with a remarkable display of energy, ingenuity, and ability. After the army was in the field he gave his personal attention to the work of the departments whose heads were at the front and attended to many of the details of the commissariat work in Bloemfontein. He frequently visited the burghers in the field and gave to them such encouragement as only the presence and praise of the leader of a nation can give to a people. In February he went to the Republican lines at Ladysmith and made an address in which he stated that Sir Alfred Milner's declaration that the power of Afrikanderism must be broken had caused the war. Several days later he was with his burghers at Kimberley, praising their valour and infusing them with renewed courage. A day or two afterward he was again in Bloemfontein, arranging for the comfort of his men and caring for the wives and children who were left behind. His duties were increased a hundred-fold as the campaign progressed, and when the first reverses came he alone of the Free Staters was able to imbue the men with new zeal. After Bloemfontein was captured by the British he transferred the capital to Kroonstad, and there, with the assistance of President Kruger, re-established the fighting spirit of the burgher army. He induced the skulking burghers to return to their compatriots at the front, and formed the plans for future resistance against the invading army. When Lord Roberts's hosts advanced from Bloemfontein, President Steyn again moved the capital and established it at Heilbron. Thereafter the capital was constantly transferred from one place to another, but through all those vicissitudes the President clung nobly to his people and country.

9. Foreigners in the War

In every war there are men who are not citizens of the country with whose army they are fighting, and the "soldier-of-fortune" is as much a recognised adjunct of modern armies as he was in the days of knight-errantry. In the American revolutionary war both the colonial and British forces were assisted by many foreigners, and in every great and small war since then the contending armies have had foreigners in their service. In the Franco-Prussian war there was a great number of foreigners, among them having been one of the British generals who took a leading part in the Natal campaign. The brief Græco-Turkish war gave many foreign officers an opportunity of securing experience, while the Spaniards in the Hispano-American war had the assistance of a small number of European officers. Even the Filipinos have had the aid of a corps of foreigners, the leader of whom, however, deserted Aguinaldo and joined the Boer forces.

There is a fascination in civilised warfare which attracts men of certain descriptions, and to them a well-fought battle is the highest form of exciting amusement. All the world is interested in warfare among human beings, and there are men who delight in fighting battles in order that their own and public interest may be gratified. It may suggest a morbid or bloodthirsty spirit, this love of warfare, but no spectacle is finer, more magnificent, than a hard-fought game in which human lives are staked against a strip of ground--a position. It is not hard to understand why many men should become fascinated with warfare and travel to the ends of the earth in order to take part in it, but a soldier of fortune needs to make no apologies. The Boer army was augmented by many of these men who delighted in war for fighting's sake, but a larger number joined the forces because they believed the Republics were fighting in a just cause.

The Boer was jealous of his own powers of generalship, and when large numbers of foreigners volunteered to lead their commandos the farmers gave a decidedly negative reply. Scores of foreign officers arrived in the country shortly after the beginning of hostilities and, intent on securing fame and experience, asked to be placed in command, but no request of that kind was granted. The Boers felt that their system of warfare was the perfect one, and they scoffed at the suggestion that European officers might teach them anything in the military line. Every foreign officer was welcomed in Pretoria and in the laagers, but he was asked to enlist as a private, or ordinary burgher. Commissions in the Boer army were not to be had for the asking, as was anticipated, and many of the foreign officers were deeply disappointed in consequence. The Boers felt that the foreigners were unacquainted with the country, the burgher mode of warfare, and lacked adroitness with the rifle, and consequently refused to place lives and battles in the hands of incompetent men. There were a few foreigners in the service of the Boers at the beginning of the war, but their number was so small as to have been without significance. Several European officers had been employed by the Governments of the Republics to instruct young Boers in artillery work--- and their instruction was invaluable--but the oft-repeated assertion that every commando was in charge of a foreign officer was as ridiculous as that of the Cape Times which stated that the British retired from Spion Kop because no water was found on its summit.

The influx of foreigners into the country began simultaneously with the war, and it continued thereafter at the rate of about four hundred men a month. The volunteers, as they were called by the burghers, consisted of the professional soldier, the man in search of loot, the man who fights for love of justice, and the adventurer. The professional soldier was of much service to the burghers so long as he was content to remain under a Boer leader, but as soon as he attempted to operate on his own responsibility he became not only an impediment to the Boers, but also a positive danger. In the early stages of the war the few foreign legions that existed met with disaster at Elandslaagte, and thereafter all the foreign volunteers were obliged to join a commando. After several months had passed the foreigners, eager to have responsible command, prevailed upon the generals to allow the formation of foreign legions to operate independently. The Legion of France, the American Scouts, the Russian Scouts, the German Corps, and several other organisations were formed, and for a month after the invest- ment of Bloemfontein these legions alone enlivened the situation by their frolicsome reports of attacks on the enemy's outposts. During those weeks the entire British army must have been put to flight scores of times at the very least, if the reports of the foreign legions may be believed, and the British casualty list must have amounted to thrice the number of English soldiers in the country. The free-rein given to the foreign legionaries was withdrawn shortly after Villebois-Mareuil and his small band of Frenchmen met with disaster at Boshof, and thereafter all the foreigners were placed under the direct command of General De la Rey.

The man in search of the spoils of war was not so numerous, but he made his presence felt by stealing whatever was portable and saleable. When he became surfeited with looting houses in conquered territory and stealing horses, luggage, and goods of lesser value in the laagers he returned to Johannesburg and Pretoria and assisted in emptying residences and stores of their contents. This style of soldier-of-fortune never went into a battle of his own accord, and when he found himself precipitated into the midst of one he lost little time in reaching a place of safety. Almost on a par with the looter was the adventurer, whose chief object of life seemed to be to tell of the battles he had assisted in winning. He was constantly in the laagers when there was no fighting in progress, but as soon as the report of a gun was heard the adventurer felt the necessity of going on urgent business to Pretoria. After the fighting he could always be depended upon to relate the wildest personal experiences that camp-fires ever heard. He could tell of amazing experiences in the wilds of South America, on the steppes of Siberia, and other ends of the earth, and after each narrative he would make a request for a "loan." The only adventures he had during the war were those which he encountered while attempting to escape from battles, and the only service he did to the Boer army was to assist in causing the disappearance of commissariat supplies.

The men who fought with the Boers because they were deeply in sympathy with the Republican cause were in far greater numbers than those with other motives, and their services were of much value to the federal forces. The majority of these were in the country when the war was begun, and were accepted as citizens of the country. They joined commandos and remained under Boer leaders during the entire campaign. In the same class were the volunteers who entered the Republics from Natal and Cape Colony, for the purpose of assisting their co-religionists and kinsmen. Of these there were about six thousand at the beginning of hostilities, but there were constant desertions, so that after the first six months of the war perhaps less than one-third of them remained. The Afrikanders of Natal and Cape Colony were not inferior in any respect to the Boers whose forces they joined, but when the tide of war changed and it became evident that the Boers would not triumph, they returned to their homes and farms

in the colonies, in order to save them from confiscation. Taking into consideration the fact that four-fifths of the white population of the two colonies was of
the same race and religion as the Boers, six thousand was not a large number of
volunteers to join the federal forces.

BATTLEFIELD OF ELANDSLAAGTE

The artillery fire of the Boer was so remarkably good that the delusion was
cherished by the British commanders that foreign artillerists were in charge of all
their guns. It was not believed that the Boers had any knowledge of arms other
than rifles, but it was not an easy matter to find a foreigner at a cannon or a
rapid-fire gun. The field batteries of the State Artillery of the Transvaal had two
German officers of low rank, who were in the country long before the war began,
but almost all the other men who assisted with the field guns were young Boers.
The heavy artillery in Natal was directed by MM. Grunberg and Leon, representatives of Creusot, who manufactured the guns. M. Leon's ability as an engineer
and gunner pleased Commandant-General Joubert so greatly that he gave him
full authority over the artillery. Major Albrecht, the director of the Free State
Artillery, was a foreigner by birth, but he became a citizen of the Free State long
before the war, and did sterling service to his country until he was captured with
Cronje at Paardeberg. Otto von Lossberg, a German-American who had seen

service in the armies of Germany and the United States, arrived in the country in March, and was thereafter in charge of a small number of heavy guns, but the majority of them were manned by Boer officers.

None of the foreigners who served in the Boer army received any compensation. They were supplied with horses and equipment, at a cost to the Boer Governments of about £35 for each volunteer, and they received better food than the burghers, but no wages were paid to them. Before a foreign volunteer was allowed to join a commando, and before he received his equipment, he was obliged to take an oath of allegiance to the Republic. Only a few men who declined to take the oath were allowed to join the army. The oath of allegiance was an adaptation of the one which caused so much difficulty between Great Britain and the Transvaal before the war. A translation of it reads--

"I hereby make an oath of solemn allegiance to the people of the South African Republic, and I declare my willingness to assist, with all my power, the burghers of this Republic in the war in which they are engaged. I further promise to obey the orders of those placed in authority according to law, and that I will work for nothing but the prosperity, the welfare, and the independence of the land and people of this Republic, so truly help me, God Almighty."

No army lists were ever to be found at Pretoria or at the front, and it was as monumental a task to secure a fair estimate of the Boer force as it was to obtain an estimate of the number of the foreigners who assisted them. The Boers had no men whom they could spare to detail to statistical work, and, in consequence, no correct figures can ever be obtained. The numerical strength of the various organisations of foreigners could readily be obtained from their commanders, but many of the foreigners were in Boer commandos, and their strength is only problematical. An estimate which was prepared by the British and American correspondents, who had good opportunities of forming as nearly a correct idea as any one, resulted in this list, which gives the numbers of those in the various organisations, as well as those in the commandos:--

Nationality	In Organisations	In Commandos
French	300	100
Hollanders	400	250
Russian	100	125
Germans	300	250
Americans	150	150
Italians	100	100
Scandinavians	100	50

Nationality	In Organisations	In Commandos
Irishmen	200	
Afrikanders		6,000
Total in Organisations	**1,650**	
Total in Commandos		**7,025**
Grand Total	**8,675**	

The French legionaries were undoubtedly of more actual service to the Boers than the volunteers of any other nationality, inasmuch as they were given the opportunities of doing valuable work. Before the war one of the large forts at Pretoria was erected by French engineers, and when the war was begun Frenchmen of military experience were much favoured by General Joubert, who was proud of his French extraction. The greater quantity of artillery had been purchased from French firms, and the Commandant-General wisely placed guns in the hands of the men who knew how to operate them well. MM. Grunberg and Leon were of incalculable assistance in transporting the heavy artillery over the mountains of Natal, and in securing such positions for them where the fire of the enemy's guns could not harm them. The work of the heavy guns, the famous "Long Toms" which the besieged in Ladysmith will remember as long as the siege itself remains in their memory, was almost entirely the result of French hands and brains, while all the havoc caused by the heavy artillery in the Natal battles was due to the engineering and gunnery of Leon, Grunberg, and their Boer assistants. After remaining in Natal until after the middle of January the two Frenchmen joined the Free State forces, to whom they rendered valuable assistance. Leon was wounded at Kimberley on February 12th, and, after assisting in establishing the ammunition works at Pretoria and Johannesburg, returned to France. Viscount Villebois-Mareuil was one of the many foreigners who joined the Boer army and lost their lives while fighting with the Republican forces. While ranking as colonel on the General Staff of the French army, and when about to be promoted to the rank of general, he resigned from the service on account of the Dreyfus affair. A month after the commencement of the war Villebois-Mareuil arrived in the Transvaal and went to the Natal front, where his military experience enabled him to give advice to the Boer generals. In January the Colonel attached himself to General Cronje's forces, with whom he took part in many engagements. He was one of the few who escaped from the disastrous fight at Paardeberg, and shortly afterwards, at the war council at Kroonstad, the French officer was created a brigadier-general--the first and only one in the Boer army--and all the foreign legions were placed in his charge. It was purposed that he should harass the enemy by attacks on their lines of communication, and it was while he was at the outset of the first of these expeditions that he and twelve of his small force of sixty men were killed at Boshof, in the north-western part of the Free State, early in April. Villebois-Mareuil was a firm believer in the final success of the Boer arms, and he received the credit of planning two battles--second Colenso and Magersfontein--which gave the Boers at least temporary success. The Viscount was a writer for the Revue des Deux Mondes, the Correspondant, and *La Liberté*, the latter of which referred to him as the latter-day Lafayette. Colonel Villebois-Mareuil was an exceptionally brave man, a fine soldier, and a gentleman whose friendship was prized.

Lieutenant Gallopaud was another Frenchman who did sterling service to the Boers while he was subordinate to Colonel Villebois-Mareuil. At Colenso Gallopaud led his men in an attack which met with extraordinary success, and later in the Free State campaign he distinguished himself by creditable deeds in several battles. Gallopaud went to the Transvaal for experience, and he secured both that and fame. After the death of Villebois-Mareuil, Gallopaud was elected commandant of the French Legion, and before he joined De la Rey's army he had the novel pleasure of subduing a mutiny among some of his men. An Algerian named Mahomed Ben Naseur, who had not been favoured with the sight of blood for several weeks, threatened to shoot Gallopaud with a Mauser, but there was a cessation of hostilities on the part of the Algerian shortly after big, powerful Gallopaud went into action.

The majority of the Hollanders who fought with the Boers were in the country when the war was begun, and they made a practical demonstration of their belief in the Boer cause by going into the field with the first commandos. The Dutch corps was under the command of Commandant Smoronberg, the former drill-master of the Johannesburg Police. Among the volunteers were many young Hollanders who had been employed by the Government in Pretoria and Johannesburg establishments, and by the Netherlands railways. In the first engagement, at Elandslaagte, in November, the corps was practically annihilated and General Kock, the leader of the Uitlander brigade, himself received his death wounds. Afterward the surviving members of the corps joined Boer commandos where stray train-loads of officers' wines, such as were found the day before the battle of Elandslaagte, were not allowed to interfere with the sobriety of the burghers. The Russian corps, under Commandant Alexis de Ganetzky and Colonel Prince Baratrion-Morgaff, was formed after all the men had been campaigning under Boer officers in Natal for several months. The majority of the men were Johannesburgers without military experience who joined the army because there was nothing else to do.

The German corps was as short-lived as the Hollander organisation, it having been part of the force which met with disaster at Elandslaagte. Colonel Schiel, a German-Boer of brief military experience, led the organisation, but was unable to display his abilities to any extent before he was made a prisoner of war. Captain Count Harran von Zephir was killed in the fight at Spion Kop, and Herr von Brusenitz was killed and Colonel von Brown was captured at the Tugela. The corps was afterward reorganised and, under the leadership of Commandant Otto Krantz of Pretoria, it fought valiantly in several battles in the Free State. Among the many German volunteers who entered the country after the beginning of hostilities was Major Baron von Reitzenstein, the winner of the renowned long-distance horseback race from Berlin to Vienna. Major von Reitzenstein was a participant in battles at Colesburg and in Natal, and was eager to remain with the Boer forces until the end of the war, but was recalled by his Government, which had granted him a leave of absence from the German army. Three of the forts at Pretoria were erected by Germans, and the large fort at Johannesburg was built by Colonel Schiel at an expense of less than £5,000.

COLONEL JOHN E. BLAKE, OF THE IRISH BRIGADE

The Americans in South Africa who elected to fight under the Boer flags did not promise to win the war single-handed, and consequently the Boers were not disappointed in the achievements of the volunteers from the sister-republic across the Atlantic. In proportion to their numbers the Americans did as well as the best volunteer foreigners, and caused the Government less trouble and expense than any of the Uitlanders' organisations. The majority of the Americans spent the first months of the war in Boer commandos, and made no effort to establish an organisation of their own, although they were of sufficient numerical strength. A score or more of them joined the Irish Brigade organised by Colonel J.E. Blake, a graduate of West Point Military Academy and a former officer in the American army, and accompanied the Brigade through the first seven months of the Natal campaign. After the exciting days of the Natal campaign John A. Hassell, an American who had been with the Vryheid commando, organised the American Scouts and succeeded in gathering what probably was the strangest body of men in the war. Captain Hassell himself was born in New Jersey, and was well educated in American public schools and the schools of experience. He spent the five years before the war in prospecting and with shooting expeditions in various parts of South Africa, and had a better idea of the geological features of the country than any of the commandants of the foreign legions. While he was with the Vryheid commando Hassell was twice wounded, once in the attack on Caesar's Hill and again at Estcourt, where he received a bayonet thrust which disabled him for several weeks and deprived him of the brief honour of being General Botha's adjutant.

The one American whose exploits will long remain in the Boer mind was John N. King, of Reading, Pennsylvania, who vowed that he would allow his hair to grow until the British had been driven from federal soil. King began his career of usefulness to society at the time of the Johnstown flood, where he and some companions lynched an Italian who had been robbing the dead. Shortly afterward he gained a deep insight into matters journalistic by being the boon companion of a newspaper man. The newspaper man was in jail on a charge of larceny; King for murder. When war was begun King was employed on a Johannesburg mine, and when his best friend determined to join the British forces he decided to enlist in the Boer army. Before parting the two made an agreement that neither should make the other prisoner in case they met. At Spion Kop, King captured his friend unawares and, after a brief conversation and a farewell grasp of the hand, King shot him dead. King took part in almost every one of the Natal battles, and when there was no fighting to do he passed the time away by such reckless exploits as going within the British firing-line at Ladysmith to capture pigs and chickens. He bore a striking resemblance to Napoleon I., and loved blood as much as the little

Corsican. When the Scouts went out from Brandfort in April and killed several of the British scouts, King wept because he had remained in camp that day and had missed the opportunity of having a part in the engagement.

The lieutenant of the Scouts was John Shea, a grey-haired man who might have had grand-children old enough to fight. Shea fought with the Boers because he thought they had a righteous cause, and not because he loved the smell of gunpowder, although he had learned to know what that was in the Spanish-American war. Shea endeavoured to introduce the American army system into the Boer army, but failed signally, and then fought side by side with old takhaars all during the Natal campaign. He was the guardian of the mascot of the scouts, William Young, a thirteen-year-old American, who was acquainted with every detail of the preliminaries of the war. William witnessed all but two of the Natal battles, and several of those in the Free State, and could relate all the stirring incidents in connection with each, but he could tell nothing more concerning his birthplace than that it was "near the shore in America," both his parents having died when he was quite young. Then there was Able-Bodied Seaman William Thompson, who was in the Wabash of the United States Navy, and served under MacCuen in the Chinese-Japanese war. Thompson and two others tried to steal a piece of British heavy artillery while it was in action at Ladysmith, but were themselves captured by some Boers who did not believe in modern miracles. Of newspaper men, there were half a dozen who laid aside the pen for the sword. George Parsons, a *Collier's Weekly* man, who was once left on a desert island on the east end of Cuba to deliver a message to Gomez, several hundred miles away; J.B. Clarke, of Webberville, Michigan, who was correspondent for a Pittsburg newspaper whenever some one could commandeer the necessary stamps; and four or five correspondents of country weeklies in Western States. Starfield and Hiley were two Texans, of American army experience, who fought with the Boers because they had faith in their cause. Starfield claimed the honour of having been pursued for half a day by two hundred British cavalryman, while Hiley, the finest marksman in the corps, had the distinction of killing Lieutenant Carron, an American, in Lord Loch's Horse, in a fierce duel behind ant-heaps at Modder River on April 21st. Later in the campaign many of the Americans who entered the country for the purpose of fighting joined Hassell's Scouts, and added to the cosmopolitan character of the organisation.

One came from Paget Sound in a sailing vessel. Another arrival boldly claimed to be the American military attaché at the Paris Exposition, and then requested every one to keep the matter a secret for fear the War Department should hear of his presence in South Africa and recall him. On the way to Africa he had a marvellous midnight experience on board ship with a masked man who shot him through one of his hands. Later the same wound was displayed as having been received at Magersfontein, Colenso, and Spion Kop. This industrious youth became adjutant to Colonel Blake, and assisted that picturesque Irish-American in securing the services of the half-hundred Red Cross men who entered the country in April.

Of the many Americans who fought in Boer commandos none did better service nor was considered more highly by the Boers than Otto von Lossberg, of New Orleans, Louisana. Lossberg was born in Germany, and received his first military training in the army of his native country. He afterwards became an American citizen, and was with General Miles' army in the Porto-Rico campaign. Lossberg arrived in the Transvaal in March, and on the last day of that month was in charge of the artillery which assisted in defeating Colonel Broadwood's column at Sannaspost. Two days later, in the fight between General Christian De Wet and McQueenies' Irish Fusiliers, Lossberg was severely wounded in the head, but a month later he was again at the front. With him continually was Baron Ernst von Wrangel, a grandson of the famous Marshal Wrangle, and who was a corporal in the American army during the Cuban war.

When one of the four sons of State Secretary Reitz who were fighting with the Boer army asked his father for permission to join the Irish Brigade, the Secretary gave an excellent description of the organisation: "The members of the Irish Brigade do their work well, and they fight remarkably well, but, my son, they are not gentle in their manner." Blake and his men were among the first to cross the Natal frontier, and their achievements were notable even if the men lacked gentility of manner. The brigade took part in almost every one of the Natal engagements and when General Botha retreated from the Tugela Colonel Blake and seventy-five of his men bravely attacked and drove back into Ladysmith a squadron of cavalry which intended to cut off the retreat of Botha's starving and exhausted burghers. Blake and his men were guarding a battery on Lombard Kop, a short distance east of Ladysmith, when he learned that Joubert was leading the retreat northward, and allowing Botha, with his two thousand men, to continue their ten days' fighting without reinforcements. Instead of retreating with the other commandos, Blake and seventy-five of his men stationed themselves on the main road between Ladysmith and Colenso and awaited the coming of Botha. A force of cavalry was observed coming out of the besieged city, and it was apparent that they could readily cut off Botha from the other Boers. Blake determined to make a bold bluff by scattering his small force over the hills and attacking the enemy from different directions. The men were ordered to fire as rapidly as possible in order to impress the British cavalry with a false idea of the size of the force. The seventy-five Irishmen and Americans made as much noise with their guns as a Boer commando of a thousand men usually did, and the result was that the cavalry wheeled about and returned into Ladysmith. Botha and his men, dropping out of their saddles from sheer exhaustion and hunger, came up from Colenso a short time after the cavalry had been driven back and made their memorable journey to Joubert's new headquarters at Glencoe. It was one of the few instances where the foreigners were of any really great assistance to the Boers.

After the relief of Ladysmith the Irish Brigade was sent to Helpmakaar Pass, and remained there for six weeks, until Colonel Blake succeeded in inducing the War Department to send them to the Free State, where these "sons of the ould sod" might make a display of their valour to the world, and more especially to Michael Davitt, who was then visiting in the country. When the Brigade was formed it was not necessary to show an Irish birth certificate in order to become a member of the organisation, and consequently there were Swedes, Russians, Germans, and Italians marching under the green flag. A half-dozen of the Brigade claimed to be Irish enough for themselves and for those who could not lay claim to such extraction, and consequently a fair mean was maintained. A second Irish Brigade was formed in April by Arthur Lynch, an Irish-Australian, who was the former Paris correspondent of a London daily newspaper. Colonel Lynch and his men were in several battles in Natal and received warm praise from the Boer generals.

The Italian Legion was commanded by a man who loved war and warfare. Camillo Richiardi and General Louis Botha were probably the two handsomest men in the army, and both were the idols of their men. Captain Richiardi had his first experience of war in Abyssinia, when he fought with the Italian army. When the Philippine war began he joined the fortunes of Aguinaldo, and became the leader of the foreign legion. For seven months he fought against the American soldiers, not because he hated the Americans, but because he loved fighting more. When the Boer war seemed to promise more exciting work Richiardi left Aguinaldo's forces and joined a Boer commando as a burgher. After studying Boer methods for several months he formed an organisation of scouts which was of great service to the army. Before the relief of Ladysmith the Italian Scouts was the ablest organisation of the kind in the Republics.

The Scandinavian corps joined Cronje's army after the outbreak of war, and took part in the battle of Magersfontein on December 11th. The corps occupied one of the most exposed positions during that battle and lost forty-five of the fifty-two men engaged. Commandant Flygare was shot in the abdomen and was being carried off the field by Captain Barendsen when a bullet struck the captain in the head and killed him instantly. Flygare extricated himself from beneath

Barendsen's body, rose, and led his men in a charge. When he had proceeded about twenty yards a bullet passed through his head, and his men leapt over his corpse only to meet a similar fate a few minutes later.

10. Boer Women in the War

One of the most glorious pages in the history of the Boer nation relates to the work of the women who fought side by side with their husbands against the hordes of murderous Zulus in the days of the early Voortrekkers. It is the story of hardy Boer women, encompassed by thousands of bloodthirsty natives, fighting over the lifeless bodies of their husbands and sons, and repelling the attacks of the savages with a spirit and strength not surpassed by the valiant burghers themselves. The magnificent heritage which these mothers of the latter-day Boer nation left to their children was not unworthily borne by the women of the end of the century, and the work which they accomplished in the war of 1899-1900 was none the less valuable, even though it was less hazardous and romantic, than that of their ancestors whose blood mingled with that of the savages on the grassy slopes of the Natal mountains.

The conspicuous part played in the war by the Boer women was but a sequence to that which they took in the political affairs of the country before the commencement of hostilities, and both were excellent demonstrations of their great patriotism and their deep loyalty to the Republics which they loved. Some one has said that real patriotism is bred only on the farms and plains of a country, and no better exemplification of the truth of the saying was necessary than that which was afforded by the wives and mothers of the burghers of the two South African Republics. Many months before the first shot of the war was fired the patriotic Boer women commenced to take an active interest in the discussion of the grave affairs of State, and it increased with such amazing rapidity and volume that they were prepared for hostilities long before the men. Women urged their husbands, fathers, and brothers to end the long period of political strife and uncertainty by shouldering arms and fighting for their independence. Even sooner than the men, the Boer women realised that peace must be broken sometime in order to secure real tranquillity in the country, and she who lived on the veld and was patriotic was anxious to have the storm come and pass as quickly as possible. So enthusiastic were the women before the war that it was a common saying among them that if the men were too timorous to fight for their liberty the daughters and grand-daughters of the heroines who fought against the Zulus at Weenen and Doornkop would take up arms.

MRS. GENERAL LUCAS J. MEYER

Even before the formal declaration of war was made, many of the Boer women prevailed upon their husbands, brothers, and sons to leave their homes and go to the borders of the Boer country to guard against any raids that might be attempted by the enemy, and in many instances women accompanied the men to prepare their meals and give them comfort. These manifestations of warlike spirit were not caused by the women's love of war, for they were even more peace-loving than the men, but they were the natural result of a desire to serve their country at a time when they considered it to be in great peril. The women knew that war would mean much bloodshed and the death of many of those whom they loved, but all those selfish considerations were laid aside when they believed that the life of their country was at stake.

For weeks preceding the commencement of hostilities farmers' wives on the veld busied themselves with making serviceable corduroy clothing, knapsacks, and bread-bags for their male relatives who were certain to go on commando; and when it became known that an ultimatum would be sent to Great Britain the women prepared the burghers' outfits, so that there would be no delay in the men's departure for the front as soon as the declaration of war should be made.

No greater or harder work was done by the women during the entire war than that which fell to their lot immediately following the formal declaration of war by the authorities. In the excitement of the occasion the Government had ne-glected to make any satisfactory arrangements for supplying the burghers with food while on the journey to the front and afterward, and consequently there was much suffering from lack of provisions and supplies. At this juncture the women came to the rescue, and in a trice they had remedied the great defect. Every farmhouse and every city residence became a bakery, and for almost two months all the bread consumed by the burgher army was prepared by the Boer women. Organisations were formed for this purpose in every city and town in the coun-try, and by means of a well-planned division of labour this improvised commis-sariat department was as effective as that which was afterward organised by the Government. Certain women baked the bread, prepared sandwiches, and boiled coffee; others procured the supplies, and others distributed the food at the various railway stations through which the commando-trains passed, or carried it directly to the laagers. One of the women who was tireless in her efforts to feed the burghers and make them comfortable as they passed through Pretoria on the railway was Mrs. F.W. Reitz, the wife of the Transvaal State Secretary, and never a commando-train passed through the capital that she was not there to distribute sandwiches, coffee, and milk.

When the first battles of the campaign had been fought and the wounded were being brought from the front the women again volunteered to relieve an embarrassed Government, and no nobler, more energetic efforts to relieve suffering were ever made than those of the patriotic daughters of the Transvaal and Orange Free State. Women from the farms assisted in the hospitals; wives who directed the herding of cattle during the absence of their husbands went to the towns and to the laager hospitals; young school girls deserted their books and assisted in giving relief to the burghers who were bullet-maimed or in the delirium of fever. No station in life was unrepresented in the humanitarian work. Two daughters of the former President of the Transvaal, the Rev. Thomas François Burgers, were nurses in the Burke hospital in Pretoria, which was established and maintained by a Boer burgher. Miss Martha Meyer, a daughter of General Lucas Meyer, devoted herself assiduously to the relief of the wounded in the same hospitals, and in the institution which Barney Barnato established in Johannesburg there were scores of young women nurses who cared for British and Boer wounded with unprejudiced attention. In every laager at the front were young Boer vrouwen who, under the protection of the Red Cross, and indifferent, to the creed, caste, or country of the wounded and dying, assuaged the suffering of those who were entrusted to their care. In the hospital-trains which carried the wounded from the battlefields to the hospitals in Pretoria and Johannesburg were Boer women who considered themselves particularly fortunate in having been able to secure posts where they could be of service, while at the stations where the trains halted were Boer women bearing baskets of fruit and bottles of milk for the unfortunate burghers and soldiers in the carriages.

When the war began and all the large mines on the Witwatersrand and all the big industries and stores in Johannesburg and Pretoria were obliged to cease operations, much distress prevailed among the poorer classes of foreigners who were left behind when the great exodus was concluded, and after a few months their poverty became most acute. Again the Boer women shouldered the burden, and in a thousand different ways relieved the suffering of those who were the innocent victims of the war. Subscription lists were opened and the wealthy Boers contributed liberally to the fund for the distressed. Depôts where the needy could secure food and clothing were established, while a soup-kitchen where Mrs. Peter Maritz Botha, one of the wealthiest women in the Republics, stood behind a table and distributed food to starving men and women, was a veritable blessing to hundreds of needy foreigners. In Johannesburg, Boer women searched through the poorest quarters of the city for families in need of food or medicine and never a needy individual was neglected. Among the few thousand British subjects who remained behind there were many who were in dire straits, but Boer women made no distinctions between friend and enemy when there was an opportunity for performing a charitable deed. Nor was their charity limited to civilians and those who were neutral in their sentiments with regard to the war. When the British prisoners of war were confined in the racecourse at Pretoria the Boer women sent many a wagon-load of fruit, luxuries, and reading matter to the soldiers who had been sent against them to deprive them of that which they esteemed most--the independence of their country. The spirit which animated the women was never better exemplified than by the action of a little Boer girl of about ten years who approached a British prisoner on the platform of the station at Kroonstaad and gave him a bottle of milk which she had kept carefully concealed under her apron. The soldier hardly had time to thank her for her gift before she turned and ran away from him as rapidly as she had the strength. It seemed as if she loved him as a man in distress, but feared him as a soldier, and hated him as the enemy of her country.

Besides assisting in the care of the wounded, the baking of bread for the burghers, and giving aid to the destitute, the women of the farms were obliged to attend to the flocks and herds which were left in their charge when the fathers, husbands, and brothers went to the front to fight. All the laborious duties of the farm were performed by the women, and it was common to witness a woman at work in the fields or driving a long ox-wagon along the roads. When the tide of war changed and the enemy drove the burghers to the soil of the Republics the work of the women became even more laborious and diversified. The widely-separated farmhouses then became typical lunch stations for the burghers, and the women willingly were the proprietresses. Boers journeying from one commando to another, or scouts and patrols on active duty, stopped at the farmhouses for food for themselves and their horses, and the women gladly prepared the finest feasts their larder afforded. No remuneration was ever accepted, and the realisation that they were giving even indirect assistance to their country's cause was deemed sufficient payment for any work performed. Certain farmhouses which were situated near frequently travelled roads became the well-known rendezvous of the burghers, and thither all the women in the neighbourhood wended their way to assist in preparing meals for them. Midway between Smaldeel and Brandfort was one of that class of farmhouses, and never a meal-time passed that Mrs. Barnard did not entertain from ten to fifty burghers. Near Thaba N'Chu was the residence of John Steyl, a member of the Free State Raad, whose wife frequently had more than one hundred burgher guests at one meal. When the battle of Sannaspost was being fought a short distance from her house, Mrs. Steyl was on one of the hills overlooking the battlefield, interspersing the watching of the progress of the battle with prayers for the success of the burghers' arms. As soon as she learned that the Boers had won the field she hastened home and prepared a sumptuous meal for her husband, her thirteen-year-old son, and all the generals who took part in the engagement.

When the winter season approached and the burghers called upon the Government for the heavy clothing which they themselves could not secure, there was another embarrassing situation, for there was only a small quantity of ready-made clothing in the country, and it was not an easy matter to secure it through the blockaded port at Delagoa Bay. There was an unlimited quantity of cloth in the country, but, as all the tailors were in the commandos at the front, the difficulty of converting the material into suits and overcoats seemed to be insurmountable until the women found a way. Unmindful of the other vast duties they were engaged in they volunteered to make the clothing, and thenceforth every Boer home was a tailor's shop. President Kruger's daughters and grand-daughters, the Misses Eloff, who had been foremost in many of the other charitable works, undertook the management of the project, and they continued to preside over the labours of several hundred women who worked in the High Court Building in Pretoria until the British forces entered the city. Thousands of suits of clothing and overcoats were made and forwarded to the burghers in the field to protect them against the rigors of the South African winter's nights.

One of the most conspicuous parts played in the war by the Boer women was that of urging their husbands and sons to abbreviate their leaves-of-absence and return to their commandos. The mothers and wives of the burghers of the Republics gave many glorious examples of their unselfishness and deep love of country, but none was of more material benefit than their efforts to preserve the strength of the army in the field. When the burghers returned to their homes on furloughs of from five days to two weeks the wives urged their immediate return, and, in many instances, insisted that they should rejoin their commandos forthwith upon pain of receiving no food if they remained at home. It was one of the Boer's absolute necessities to have a furlough every two or three months, and unless it was given to him by the officers he was more than likely to take it without the prescribed permission. When burghers without such written permits reached their homes they were not received by their wives with the customary cordiality, and the air of frigidity which encompassed them soon compelled them to return to the field. The Boer women despised a coward, or a man who seemed to be shirking his duty to his country, and, not unlike their sisters in countries of older civilisation, they possessed the power of expressing their disapprobation of such acts. It was not uncommon for the women to threaten to take their husbands' post of duty if the men insisted upon remaining at home, and invariably the ruse was efficient in securing the burghers' early return.

During the war there were many instances to prove that the Boer women of the end of the century inherited the bravery and heroic fortitude of their ancestors who fell victims to the Zulu assegais in the Natal valley, in 1838. The Boer women were as anxious to take an active part in the campaign as their grand-mothers were at Weenen, and it was only in obedience to the rules formulated by the officers that Amazon corps were absent from the commandos. Instances were not rare of women trespassing these regulations, and scores of Boer women can claim the distinction of having taken part in many bloody battles. Not a few yielded up their life's blood on the altar of liberty, and many will carry the scars of bullet-wounds to the grave.

In the early part of the campaign there was no military rule which forbade women journeying to the front, and in consequence the laagers enjoyed the presence of many of the wives and daughters of the burghers. Commandant-General Joubert set an example to his men by having Mrs. Joubert continually with him on his campaigning trips, and the burghers were not slow in patterning after him. While the greater part of the army lay around besieged Ladysmith large numbers of women were in the laagers, and they were continually busying themselves with the preparation of food for their relatives and with the care of the sick and wounded. Not infrequently did the women accompany their hus-bands to the trenches along the Tugela front, and it was asserted, with every evidence of veracity, that many of them used the rifles against the enemy with even more ardour and precision than the men. On February 28th, while the fighting around Pieter's Hills was at its height, the British forces captured a Boer woman of nineteen years who had been fatally wounded. Before she died she stated that she had been fighting from the same trench with her husband, and that he had been killed only a few minutes before a bullet struck her.

While the Boer army was having its many early successes in Natal few of the women partook in the actual warfare from choice, or because they believed that it was necessary for them to fight. The majority of those who were in the engagements happened to be with their husbands when the battles were begun, and had no opportunity of escaping. The burghers objected to the presence of women within the firing lines, and every effort was made to prevent them from being in dangerous localities, but when it was impossible to transfer them to places of safety during the heat of the battle there was no alternative but to provide them with rifles and bandoliers so that they might protect themselves. The half-hundred women who endured the horrors of the siege at Paardeberg with Cronje's small band of warriors chose to remain with their husbands and brothers when Lord Roberts offered to convey them to places of safety, but they were in no wise an impediment to the burghers, for they assisted in digging trenches and wielded the carbines as assiduously as the most energetic men.

MRS. OTTO KRANTZ, A BOER AMAZON

One of the women who received the Government's sanction to join a commando was Mrs. Otto Krantz, the wife of a professional hunter. Mrs. Krantz accompanied her husband to Natal at the commencement of hostilities, and remained in the field during almost the entire campaign in that colony. In the battle of Elandslaagte, where some of the hardest hand-to-hand fighting of the war occurred, this Amazon was by the side of her husband in the thick of the engagement, but escaped unscathed. Later she took part in the battles along the Tugela, and when affairs in the Free State appeared to be threatening she was one of the first to go to the scene of action in that part of the country.

Among the prisoners captured by the British forces at Colesburg were three Boer women who wore men's clothing, but it was not until after they had been confined in the prison-ship at Cape Town for several weeks that their sex was discovered. A real little Boertje was Helena Herbst Wagner, of Zeerust, who spent five months in the laagers and in the trenches without her identity being revealed. Her husband went to the field early in the war and left her alone with a baby. The infant died in January and the disconsolate woman donned her husband's clothing, obtained a rifle and bandolier, and went to the Natal front to search for her soldier-spouse. Failing to find him, she joined the forces of Commandant Ben Viljoen and faced bullets, bombs, and lyddite at Spion Kop, Pont Drift, and Pieter's Hills. During the retreat to Van Tonder's Nek the young woman learned that her husband lay seriously wounded in the Johannesburg hospital, and she deserted the army temporarily to nurse him.

When Louis Botha became Commandant-General of the army he issued an order that women would not be permitted to visit the laagers, and few, if any, took part in the engagements for some time thereafter. When the forces of the enemy approached Pretoria the women made heroic efforts to encourage the burghers, and frequently went to the laagers to cheer them to renewed resistance. Mrs. General Botha and Mrs. General Meyer were specially energetic and effective in their efforts to instil new courage in the men, and during the war there was no scene which was more edifying than that of those two patriotic Boer women riding about the laagers and beseeching the burghers not to yield to despair.

On the fifteenth of May more than a thousand women assembled in the Government Buildings at Pretoria for the purpose of deciding upon a course of action in the grave crisis which confronted the Republic. It was the gravest assemblage that was ever gathered together in that city--a veritable concourse of Spartan mothers. There was little speech, for the hearts of all were heavy, and tears were more plentiful than words, but the result of the meeting was the best testimonial of its value.

It was determined to ask the Government to send to the front all the men who were employed in the Commissariat, the Red Cross, schools, post and telegraph offices, and to fill the vacancies thus created with women. A memorial, signed by Mrs. H.S. Bosman, Mrs. General Louis Botha, Mrs. F. Eloff, Mrs. P.M.

Botha, and Mrs. F.W. Reitz, was adopted for transmission to the Government asking for permission to make such changes in the commissariat and other departments, and ending with these two significant clauses:--

1.--A message of encouragement will be sent to our burghers who are at the front, beseeching them to present a determined stand against the enemy in the defence of our sacred cause, and pointing out to those who are losing heart the terrible consequences which will follow should they prove weak and wanting in courage at the present crisis in our affairs.

2.--The women throughout the whole State are requested to provide themselves with weapons, in the first instance to be employed in self-defence, and secondly so that they may be in a position to place themselves entirely at the disposition of the Government.

The last request was rather superfluous in view of the fact that the majority of the women in the Transvaal were already provided with arms. There was hardly a Boer homestead which was not provided with enough rifles for all the members of the family, and there were but few women who were not adepts in the use of firearms. In Pretoria a woman's shooting club was organised at the outset of the war, and among the best shots were the Misses Eloff, the President's grand-daughters; Mrs. Van Alphen, the wife of the Postmaster-General, and Mrs. Reitz, the wife of the State Secretary. The object of the organisation was to train the members in the use of the rifle so that they might defend the city against the enemy. The club members took great pride in the fact that Mrs. Paul Kruger was the President of the organisation, and it was mutually agreed that the aged woman should be constantly guarded by them in the event of Pretoria being besieged. Happily the city was not obliged to experience that horror, and the club members were spared the ordeal of protecting President and Mrs. Kruger with their rifles as they had vowed to do.

The Boer women endured many discomforts, suffered many griefs, and bore many heartaches on account of the war and its varying fortunes, but throughout it all they acted bravely. There were no wild outbursts of grief when fathers, husbands, brothers or sons were killed in battle, and no untoward exclamations of joy when one of them earned distinction in the field. Reverses of the army were made the occasions for a renewed display of patriotism or the signal for the sending of another relative to the field. Unselfishness marked all the works of the woman of the city or veld, and the welfare of the country was her only ambition. She might have had erroneous opinions concerning the justice of the war and the causes which were responsible for it, but she realised that the land for which her mother and her grandmother had wept and bled and for which all those whom she loved were fighting and dying was in distress, and she was patriotic enough to offer herself for a sacrifice on her country's altar.

MRS. COMMANDANT-GENERAL LOUIS BOTHA

11. Incidents of the War

In every battle, and even in a day's life in the laagers, there were multitudes of interesting incidents as only such a war produces, and although Sherman's saying that "War is hell" is as true now as it ever was, there was always a plenitude of amusing spectacles and events to lighten the burdens of the fighting burghers. There were the sad sides of warfare, as naturally there would be, but to these the men in the armies soon became hardened, and only the amusing scenes made any lasting impression upon their minds. It was strange that when a burgher during a battle saw one of his fellow-burghers killed in a horrible manner, and witnessed an amusing runaway, that after the battle he should relate the details of the latter and say nothing of the former, but such was usually the case. Men came out of the bloody Spion Kop fight and related amusing incidents of the struggle, and never touched upon the grave phases until long afterward when their fund of laughable experiences was exhausted. After the battle of Sannaspost the burghers would tell of nothing but the amusing manner in which the drivers of the British transport wagons acted when they found that they had fallen into the hands of the Boers in the bed of the spruit and the fun they had in pursuing the fleeing cavalrymen. At the ending of almost every battle there was some conspicuous amusing incident which was told and retold and laughed about until a new and fresh incident came to light to take its place.

In one of the days' fighting at Magersfontein a number of youthful Boers, who were in their first battle, allowed about one hundred Highlanders to approach to within a hundred yards of the trench in which they were concealed, and then sprang up and shouted: "Hands up!" The Highlanders were completely surprised, promptly threw down their arms, and advanced with arms above their heads. One of the young Boers approached them, then called his friends, and, scratching his head, asked: "What shall we do with them?" There was a brief consultation, and it was decided to allow the Highlanders to return to their column. When the young burghers arrived at the Boer laager with the captured rifles and bandoliers, General Cronje asked them why they did not bring the men. The youths looked at each other for a while; then one replied, rather sheepishly, "We did not know they were wanted." In the same battle an old Boer had his first view of the quaintly dressed Highlanders, and at a distance mistook them for a herd of ostriches from a farm that was known to be in the neighbourhood, refused to fire upon them, and persuaded all the burghers in his and the neighbouring trenches that they were ostriches and not human beings.

During the second battle at Colenso a large number of Boers swam across the river and captured thirty or forty British soldiers who had lost the way and had taken refuge in a sloot. An old takhaar among the Boers had discarded almost all his clothing before entering the river, and was an amusing spectacle in shirt, bandolier, and rifle. One of the soldiers went up to the takhaar, looked at him from head to foot, and, after saluting most servilely, inquired, "To what regiment do you belong, sir?" The Boer returned the salute, and, without smiling, replied, "I am one of Rhodes' 'uncivilised Boers,' sir." In the same fight an ammunition wagon, heavily laden, and covered with a huge piece of duck, was in an exposed position, and attracted the fire of the British artillery. General Meyer and a number of burghers were near the wagon, and were waiting for a lull in the bombardment in order to take the vehicle to a place of safety. They counted thirty-five shells that fell around the wagon without striking it, and then the firing ceased. Several men were sent forward to move the vehicle, and when they were within several yards of it two Blacks crept from under the duck covering, shook themselves, and walked away as if nothing had interrupted their sleep.

In the Pretoria commando there was a young professional photographer named Reginald Shepperd who carried his camera and apparatus with him during the greater part of the campaign, and took photographs whenever he had an opportunity. On the morning of the Spion Kop fight, when the burghers were preparing to make the attack on the enemy, Mr. Shepperd gathered all the burghers of the Carolina laager and posed them for a photograph. He was on the point of exposing the plate when a shrapnel shell exploded above the group, and every one fled. The camera was left behind and all the men went into the battle. In the afternoon when the engagement had ended it was found that another shell had torn off one of the legs of the camera's tripod and that forty-three of the men who were in the group in the morning had been killed or wounded. Before the same battle, General Schalk Burger asked Mr. Shepperd to photograph him, as he had had a premonition of death, and stated that he desired that his family should have a good likeness of him. The General was in the heat of the fight, but he was not killed.

While Ladysmith was being besieged by the Boers there were many interesting incidents in the laagers of the burghers, even if there was little of exciting interest. In the Staats Artillery there were many young Boers who were constantly inventing new forms of amusement for themselves and the older burghers, and some of the games were as hazardous as they seemed to be interesting to the participants.

The "Long Tom" on Bulwana Hill was fired only when the burghers were in the mood, but occasionally the artillery youths desired to amuse themselves, and then they operated the gun as rapidly as its mechanism would allow. When the big gun had been discharged, the young Boers were wont to climb on the top of the sandbags behind which it was concealed, and watch for the explosion of the shell in Ladysmith. After each shot from the Boer gun it was customary for the British to reply with one or more of their cannon and attempt to dislodge "Long Tom." After seeing the flash of the British guns the burghers on the sandbags waited until they heard the report of the explosion, then called out, "I spy!" as a warning that the shell would be coming along in two or three seconds, and quietly jumped down behind the bags, while the missile passed over their retreats. It was a dangerous game, and the old burghers frequently warned them against playing it, but they continued it daily, and no one was ever injured. The men who operated the British and Boer heliographs at the Tugela were a witty lot, and they frequently held long conversations with each other when there were no messages to be sent or received by their respective officers. In February the Boer operator signalled to the British operator on the other side of the river and asked: "When is General Buller coming over here for that Christmas dinner? It is becoming cold and tasteless." The good-natured Briton evaded the question and questioned him concerning the date of Paul Kruger's coronation as King of South Africa. The long-distance conversation continued in the same vein, each operator trying to have amusement at the expense of the other. What probably was the most mirth-provoking communication between the two combatants in the early part of the campaign was the letter which Colonel Baden-Powell sent to General Snyman, late in December, and the reply to it. Colonel Baden-Powell, in his letter, which was several thousand words in length, told his besieger that it was utter folly for the Boers to continue fighting such a great power as Great Britain, that the British army was invincible, that the Boers were fighting for an unjust cause, and that the British had the sympathy of the American nation. General Snyman made a brief reply, the gist of which was, "Come out and fight."

GENERAL SNYMAN

A British nobleman, who was captured by the Boers at the Moester's Hoek fight in the Free State in April, was the author of a large number of communications which were almost as mirthful as Colonel Baden-Powell's effort. When he was made a prisoner of war the Earl had a diary filled with the most harrowing personal experiences ever penned, and it was chiefly on that evidence that General De Wet sent him with the other prisoners to Pretoria. The Earl protested against being sent to Pretoria, asserting that he was a war correspondent and a non-combatant, and dispatched most pitiful telegrams to Presidents Kruger and Steyn, State Secretary Reitz and a host of other officials, demanding an instant release from custody. In the telegrams he stated that he was a peer of the realm; that all doubts on that point could be dispelled by a reference to Burke's Peerage; that he was not a fighting-man; that it would be disastrous to his reputation as a correspondent if he were not released in order that he might cable an exclusive account of the Moester's Hoek battle to his newspaper, and finally ended by demanding his instant release and safe conduct to the British lines. The Boers installed the Earl in the officers' prison, and printed his telegrams in the newspapers, with the result that the Briton was the most laughed-at man that appeared in the Boer countries during the whole course of the war.

Several days before Commandant-General Joubert died he related an amusing story of an Irishman who was taken prisoner in one of the Natal battles. The Irishman was slightly wounded in one of his hands and it was decided to send him to the British lines together with all the other wounded prisoners, but he refused to be sent back. After he had protested strenuously to several other Boer officers, the soldier was taken before General Joubert, who pointed out to him the advantages of being with his own people and the discomforts of a military prison. The Irishman would not waver in his determination and finally exclaimed: "I claim my rights as a prisoner of war and refuse to allow myself to be sent back. I have a wife and two children in Ireland, and I know what is good for my health." The man was so obdurate, General Joubert said, that he could do nothing but send him to the Pretoria military prison. An incident of an almost similar nature occurred at the battle of Sannaspost, where the Boers captured almost two hundred wagons.

Among the convoy was a Red Cross ambulance wagon filled with rifles and a small quantity of ammunition. The Boers unloaded the wagon and then informed the physician in charge of it that he might proceed and rejoin the column to which he had been attached. The physician declined to move and explained his action by saying that he had violated the rules of the International Red Cross and would therefore consider himself and his assistants prisoners of war. General Christian De Wet would not accept them as prisoners and trekked southward, leaving them behind to rejoin the British column several days afterward.

FIRST BRITISH PRISONERS OF WAR CAPTURED NEAR DUNDEE

During the war it was continually charged by both combatants that dum-dum bullets were being used, and undoubtedly there was ample foundation for the charges. Both Boers and British used that particular kind of expansive bullet notwithstanding all the denials that were made in newspapers and orations. After the battle of Pieter's Hills, on February 28th, Dr. Krieger, General Meyer's Staff Physician, went into General Sir Charles Warren's camp for the purpose of exchanging wounded prisoners. After the interchange of prisoners had been accomplished General Warren produced a dum-dum bullet which had been found on a dead Boer's body and, showing it to Dr. Krieger, asked him why the Boers used the variety of cartridge that was not sanctioned by the rules of civilised warfare. Dr. Krieger took the cartridge in his hand and, after examining it, returned it to Sir Charles with the remark that it was a British Lee-Metford dum-dum. General Warren seemed to be greatly nonplussed when several of his officers confirmed the physician's statement and informed him that a large stock of dum-dum cartridges had been captured by the Boers at Dundee. It is an undeniable fact that the Boers captured thousands of rounds of dum-dum cartridges which bore the "broad arrow" of the British army, and used them in subsequent battles. It was stated in Pretoria that the Boers had a small stock of dum-dum ammunition, which was not sent to the burghers at the front at the request of President Kruger, who strongly opposed the use of an expansive bullet in warfare. It was an easy matter, however, for the Boers to convert their ordinary Mauser cartridges into dum-dum by simply cutting off the point of the bullet, and this was occasionally done.

One of the pluckiest men in the Boer army was Arthur Donnelly, a young Irish American from San Francisco, who served in the Pretoria detective force for several years, and went to the war in one of the commandos under General Cronje. At the battle of Koedoesberg Donnelly and Captain Higgins, of the Duke of Cornwall's regiment, both lay behind ant-heaps, several hundred yards apart, and engaged in a duel with carbines for almost an hour. After Donnelly had fired seventeen shots Captain Higgins was fatally wounded by a bullet, and lifted his handkerchief in token of surrender. When the young Irish-American reached him the officer was bleeding profusely, and started to say: "You were a better man than I," but he died in Donnelly's arms before he could utter the last two words of the sentence. At Magersfontein Donnelly was in a perilous position between the two forces, and realised that he could not escape being captured by the British. He saw a number of cavalrymen sweeping down upon him, and started to run in an opposite direction. Before he had proceeded a long distance he stumbled across the corpse of a Red Cross physician which lay partly concealed under tall grass. In a moment Donnelly had exchanged his own papers and credentials for those in the physician's pockets, and a minute later the cavalrymen were upon him. He was sent to Cape Town, and confined in the prison-ship Manila, from which he and two other Boers attempted to escape on New Year's night. One of the men managed to reach the water without being observed by the guards, and swam almost three miles to shore, but Donnelly and the other prisoner did not succeed in their project. Several days later he was released on account of his Red Cross credentials, and was sent to the British front to be delivered to the Boer commander. He was taken out under a flag of truce by several unarmed British officers, and several armed Boers went to receive him. While the transfer was being made a British horseman, with an order to the officers to hold the prisoner, dashed up to the group and delivered his message. The officers attempted to take Donnelly back to camp with them, but he refused to go, and, taking one of the Boer's rifles, ordered them to return without him--a command which they obeyed with alacrity in view of the fact that all of them were unarmed, while the Boers had carbines.

When the British column under Colonel Broadwood left the village of Thaba N'Chu on March 30th all the British inhabitants were invited to accompany the force to Bloemfontein, where they might have the protection of a stronger part of the army. Among those who accepted the invitation were four ladies and four children, ranging in ages from sixteen months to fifteen years. When the column was attacked by the Boers at Sannaspost the following morning, the ladies and children were sent by the Boers to a culvert in the incomplete railway line which crossed the battlefield, and remained there during almost the entire battle. They were in perfect safety, so far as being actually in the line of fire was concerned, but bullets and shells swept over and exploded near them, and they were in constant terror of being killed. The nervous tension was so great and continued for such a long time that one of the children, a twelve-year-old daughter of Mrs. J. Shaw McKinlay, became insane shortly after the battle was ended.

An incident of the same fight was a duel between two captains of the opposing forces. In the early parts of the engagement the burghers and the soldiers were so close together that many hand-to-hand encounters took place and many a casualty followed. Captain Scheppers, of the Boer heliographers, desired to make a prisoner of a British captain and asked him to surrender. The British officer said that he would not be captured alive, drew his sword, and attempted to use it. The Boer grasped the blade, wrenched the sword from the officer's hand, and knocked him off his horse. The Briton fired several revolver shots at Scheppers while the Boer was running a short distance for his carbine, but missed him. After Scheppers had secured his rifle the two fired five or six shots at each other at a range of about ten yards and, with equal lack of skill, missed. Finally, Scheppers hit the officer in the chest and laid him low. At the same time near the same spot two Boers called upon a recruit in Roberts's Horse to surrender, but the young soldier was so thoroughly frightened that he held his rifle perpendicularly in front of him and emptied the magazine toward the clouds.

While the siege of Ladysmith was in progress, Piet Boueer, of the Pretoria commando, made a remarkable shot which was considered as the record during the Natal campaign. He and several other Boers were standing on one of the hills near the laager when they observed three British soldiers emerging from one of the small forts on the outskirts of the city. The distance was about 1,400 yards, or almost one mile, but Boueer fired at the men, and the one who was walking between the others fell. The two fled to the fort, but returned to the spot a short time afterward, and the Boer fired at them a second time. The bullet raised a small cloud of dust between the men, sent them back again, and they did not return until night for their companion, who had undoubtedly been killed by the first shot. There were many other excellent marksmen in the Boer army, whose ability was often demonstrated in the interims of battles. After 1897, shooting clubs were organised at Pretoria, Potchefstroom, Krugersdorp, Klerksdorp, Johannesburg and Heidelberg, and frequent contests were held between the various organisations. In the last contest before the war E. Blignaut, of Johannesburg, won the prize by making one hundred and three out of a possible one hundred and five points, the weapon having been a Mauser at a range of seven hundred yards. These contests, naturally, developed many fine marksmen, and, in consequence, it was not considered an extraordinary feat for a man to kill a running hare at five hundred yards. While the Boers were waiting for Lord Roberts's advance from Bloemfontein, Commandant Blignaut, of the Transvaal, killed three running springbok at a range of more than 1,700 yards, a feat witnessed by a score of persons.

The Boers were not without their periods of depression during the war, but when these had passed there was no one who laughed more heartily over their actions during those times than they. The first deep gloom that the Boers experienced was after the three great defeats at Paardeberg, Kimberley and Ladysmith, and the minor reverses at Abraham's Kraal, Poplar Grove and Bloemfontein. It was amusing, yet pitiful, to see an army lose all control of itself and flee like a wild animal before a forest fire. As soon as the fight at Poplar Grove was lost the burghers mounted their horses and fled northward. President Kruger and the officers could do nothing but follow them. They passed through Bloemfontein and excited the population there; then, evading roads and despising railway transportation, they rode straight across the veld and never drew rein until they reached Brandfort, more than thirty miles from Poplar Grove. Hundreds did not stop even at Brandfort, but continued over the veld until they reached their homes in the north of the Free State and in the Transvaal. In their alarm they destroyed all the railway bridges and tracks as far north as Smaldeel, sixty miles from Bloemfontein, and made their base at Kroonstad, almost forty miles farther north. A week later a small number of the more daring burghers sallied toward Bloemfontein and found that not a single British soldier was north of that city. So fearful were they of the British army before the discovery of their foolish flight that two thousand cavalrymen could have sent them all across the Vaal river.

12. APPENDIX - The Strength of the Boer Army

The War Departments of the two Boer Governments never made any provision for obtaining statistics concerning the strength of the armies in the field, and consequently the exact number of burghers who bore arms at different periods of the war will never be accurately known. A year before the war was begun the official reports of the two Governments stated that the Transvaal had thirty thousand and the Free State ten thousand men between the ages of sixteen and sixty, capable of performing military duties, but these figures proved to be far in excess of the number of men who were actually bearing arms at any one period of the war. In the early stages of the war men who claimed to have intimate knowledge of Boer affairs estimated the strength of the Republican armies variously from sixty thousand to more than one hundred thousand men. Major Laing, who had years of South African military experience, and became a member of Field-Marshal Lord Roberts's bodyguard, in December estimated the strength of the Boer forces at more than one hundred thousand men, exclusive of the foreigners who joined the fortunes of the Republican armies. Other men proved, with wondrous arrays of figures and statistics, that the Boer army could not possibly consist of less than eighty or ninety thousand men.

The real strength of the Boer armies at no time exceeded thirty thousand armed men, and of that number more than one-half were never in the mood for fighting. If it could be ascertained with any degree of accuracy it would be found that not more than fifteen thousand Boers were ever engaged in battles, while the other half of the army remained behind in the laagers and allowed those who were moved by the spirit or by patriotism to volunteer for waging battles. As has been pointed out in other chapters, the officers had no power over their men, and consequently the armies were divided into two classes of burghers: those who volunteered their services whenever there was a battle, and those who remained in the laagers--the "Bible-readers," as they were called by some of the more youthful Boers. There were undoubtedly more than thirty thousand men in the Republics capable of bearing arms, but it was never possible to compel all of them to go to the front, nor was it less difficult to retain them there when once they had reached the commando-laagers. Ten per cent. of the men in the commandos were allowed to return to their homes on leave of absence, and about an equal proportion left the laagers without permission, so that the officers were never able to keep their forces at their normal strength.

The War Departments at Pretoria and Bloemfontein and the officers of the commandos at the front had no means of learning the exact strength of the forces in the field except by making an actual enumeration of the men in the various commandos, and this was never attempted. There were no official lists in either of the capitals and none of the commandos had even a roll-call, so that to obtain a really accurate number of burghers in the field it was necessary to visit all the commandos and in that way arrive at a conclusion.

Early in December the Transvaal War Department determined to make a Christmas gift to all the burghers of the two Republics who were in the field, and all the generals and commandants were requested to send accurate lists of the number of men in their commands. Replies were received from every commando, and the result showed that there were almost twenty-eight thousand men in the field. That number of presents was forwarded, and on Christmas day every burgher at the front received one gift, but there were almost two thousand packages undistributed. This was almost conclusive proof that the Boer armies in December did not exceed twenty-six thousand men.

At various times during the campaign the foreign newspaper correspondents--Mr. Douglas Story, of the London *Daily Mail*; Mr. John O. Knight, of the *San Francisco Call*; Mr. Thomas F. Millard, of the New York Herald, and the writer--made strenuous efforts to secure accurate information concerning the Boers' strength, and the results invariably showed that there were less than thirty thousand men in the field. The correspondents visited all the principal commandos and had the admirable assistance of the generals and commandants, as well as that of the officers of the War Departments, but frequently the results did not rise above the twenty-five thousand mark. According to the statement of the late Commandant-General Joubert, made several days before his death, he never had more than thirteen thousand men in Natal, and of that number less than two thousand were engaged in the trek to Mooi River. After the relief of Ladysmith the forces in Natal dwindled down, by reason of desertions and withdrawals, to less than five thousand, and when General Buller began his advance there were not more than four thousand five hundred Boers in that Colony to oppose him.

The strength of the army in the field varied considerably, on account of causes which are described elsewhere, and there is no doubt that it frequently fell below twenty thousand men while the Boers were still on their enemy's territory. The following table, prepared with great care and with the assistance of the leading Boer commanders, gives as correct an idea of the burghers' numerical strength actually in the field at various stages of the campaign as will probably ever be formulated:--

Date	Natal	Free State and Border	Transvaal and Border	Total
November 1, 1899	12,000	12,000	5,000	29,000
December 1, 1899	13,000	12,000	5,000	30,000
January 1, 1900	13,000	12,000	3,000	28,000
February 1, 1900	12,000	10,000	3,000	25,000
March 1, 1900	8,000	8,000	7,000	23,000
April 1, 1900	5,000	10,000	10,000	25,000
May 1, 1900	4,500	9,000	9,000	22,500
June 1, 1900	0	4,500	16,000	20,500
July 1, 1900	0	4,000	15,000	19,000

According to this table, the average strength of the Boer forces during the nine months was considerably less than 25,000 men. In refutation of these figures it may be found after the conclusion of hostilities that a far greater number of men surrendered their guns to the British army, but it must be remembered that not every Boer who owned a weapon was continually in the field.

CPSIA information can be obtained
at www.ICGtesting.com
Printed in the USA
LVOW03s1521141217
559733LV00012B/1036/P